Advance Prais

"No one is better qualified __ _____ ____ _____ _____, ____ __
activist-scholar Curtiss Paul DeYoung. His works have fueled the faith
and provided a compass for Christian activists nationally and globally. . . .
This new book gave me ecstatic motivation and creative first-time
insights, which made the ancient text alive and more relevant than the
morning news. . . . This book is the answer for all who experience social
justice burn-out and discouragement. It reignites the transformative relationship with the living God who calls us to love mercy and do justly. You
cannot read this book as I did and remain the same. . . . The end notes of
each chapter provide an updated theological education for persons seeking an informed faith. This book is one of the most moving and powerful books that I have read in the past year."

—J. Alfred Smith Sr., Pastor Emeritus,
Allen Temple Baptist Church, Oakland CA,
Professor Emeritus Berkeley School of Theology, Berkeley, CA

"The world needs activist preachers, and Curtiss DeYoung summons
them forth with a rousing wake-up call in this extremely relevant book!
The Risk of Being Woke challenges people of faith to intentionally
intersect the pulpit with the streets by working towards a vision of a just
society that is deeply rooted in God and Scripture. If you're ready to
restore the credibility of the church in this generation by putting your
commitment to racial justice into action, this book is for you. I highly
recommend it!"

—Dr. Brenda Salter McNeil, Salter McNeil & Associates, Author

"*The Risk of Being Woke* is another relevant and impactful book by
Christian ethicist and public theologian Curtiss Paul DeYoung for all who
are committed to racial justice activism. This scholarly yet accessible
resource of sermonic analysis and reflections will stir and nurture faith-
inspired activists, pastors, preachers, teachers, and readers in their oratorical assignments and callings."

—Gina M. Stewart, Senior Pastor,
Christ Missionary Baptist Church-Memphis,
Tennessee, and President-Lott Carey Foreign Mission Convention

"My friend and brother Curtiss Paul DeYoung is that unique blend of
proponent and practitioner, one who says and does, who talks and walks.

This latest literary offering from the pen of Dr. DeYoung calls and challenges us to 'wokeness' of the best kind and does it through a Biblical lens. In this book, we see the mind of a scholar and the heart of a shepherd. As such, it offers a much-needed perspective in this day and time. I pray that this book wakes us up and spurs us to action."

—Bishop Timothy J. Clarke

"DeYoung's collection of sermonic reflections is rich in practical wisdom honed through decades of faith-based activism. Fighting systemic injustice carries risks, but it is biblically mandated and grounded in the goodness of God. Readers will find here food for the long, hard, joyful journey toward beloved community."

—Edgardo A. Colón-Emeric, Dean of the Divinity School, Irene and William McCutchen Professor of Reconciliation and Theology, Director, Center for Reconciliation, Duke University Divinity School

"This text is a witness's open reflections for those white activists who care to learn how to risk being a 'woke' follower of Jesus Christ in these turbulent times. The book is a compilation of sermonic reflections that span the evolution over a lifetime of becoming and being a white activist engaged in the struggle for racial justice and healing past and present wounds. . . . The reflections provide lessons in reading and re-reading the Biblical texts in a way that provides a map, even a guide, for faithful disciples to preach, teach, pray, and act for racial justice and healing. It is clear, however, that to embrace any of the lessons laid out here is to *risk*, to risk being 'attentive to your surroundings, to the world, to injustices, to suffering,' to *Risk Being Woke!*"

—Dr. Addie Lorraine Walker, SSND, Director, Sankofa Institute for African American Pastoral Leadership, Oblate School of Theology, San Antonio, Texas

"This compelling collection of sermons grounds the struggle for racial justice in the teachings of Scripture, the lives of the prophets, and the example of Jesus, thus providing desperately needed spiritual sustenance to help activists for racial and social justice stay in the fight. I highly recommend this book to every Christian who understands that their faith calls them to build the kingdom of God here on Earth."

—Rev. Adam Russell Taylor, President of Sojourners

THE RISK OF BEING
WOKE

Sermonic Reflections for Activists

Curtiss Paul DeYoung

Foreword by Iva E. Carruthers

JUDSON PRESS
PUBLISHERS SINCE 1824
VALLEY FORGE, PA

Judson Press has made every effort to trace the ownership of all quotes. In the event of a question arising from the use of a quote, we regret any error made and will be pleased to make the necessary correction in future printings and editions of this book.

Unless otherwise indicated, Scripture quotations are taken from the New Revised Standard Version Updated Edition. Copyright© 2021 National Council of Churches of Christ in the United States of America. Used by permission. All rights reserved worldwide. Scripture quotations marked NIV are from the New International Version, Inclusive Language edition (London: Hodder & Stoughton, 1996).

Interior design by Wendy Ronga.
Cover design by Lisa Cain.

Library of Congress Cataloging-in-Publication data
Names: DeYoung, Curtiss Paul, author. Title: The risk of being woke: sermonic reflections for activists / Curtiss Paul DeYoung.
Description: Valley Forge, PA: Judson Press, 2023. | Includes bibliographical references. Identifiers: LCCN 2022046839 (print) | LCCN 2022046840 (ebook) | ISBN 9780817018436 (paperback) | ISBN 9780817082512 (epub) Subjects: LCSH: Race relations—Religious aspects—Christianity—Sermons. | Sermons, American—21st century. Classification: LCC BT734.2 .D52 2023 (print) | LCC BT734.2 (ebook) | DDC 277.308/3089—dc23/eng/20230126
LC record available at https://lccn.loc.gov/2022046839
LC ebook record available at https://lccn.loc.gov/2022046840

Printed in the U.S.A.
First printing, 2023.

Contents

Foreword

The Risk of Being Woke: Sermonic Reflections for Activists is a wisdom text and serves as a soul protector for faithful activists in any season of the journey towards justice. The book chronicles 21st-century events that shaped the nature of justice activists' struggle and resistance. Bundled as an enduring sermonic call, Curtiss P. DeYoung offers us libations watered in the Biblical texts and ancestral memories that call and strengthen us to steadfast ministries of liberation, affirmation, and transformation.

DeYoung begins by reminding us that "Lazarus was sentenced to death because Jesus woke him up" (John 11:11). He also reminds us that *woke* was used as early as the 1930s in the African American community as a warning to stay alert in the face of racism; and, in 2014, Black Lives Matter activists used woke in reference to police shootings during the Ferguson protests."

DeYoung's *The Risk of Being Woke* lays out an unabashed connection of staying woke to the process of revolution. Many know of Rev. Dr. Martin Luther King's "I Have a Dream"—his most popularized speech. Fewer likely know of his memorable 1965 commencement speech at Oberlin College titled, "Remaining Awake Through a Great Revolution," in which he popularized a theological reflection on the narrative of Rip Van Winkle:

> "...the most striking fact about the story of Rip Van Winkle is not that he slept 20 years, but that he slept through a revolution...There is nothing more tragic than to sleep through a revolution... The great challenge...today

is to remain awake through this social revolution...Never allow it to be said that you are silent onlookers, detached spectators, but that you are involved participants in the struggle to make justice a reality."[1]

An even lesser-known fact is that the Oberlin address's framework originated six years before, given by Rev. Dr. King at Morehouse College's commencement in June 1959. There, he told the African American graduates:

> "If you go home, sit down, and do nothing about the revolution which we are witnessing you will be the victim of a dangerous optimism. ...the great problem confronting man today is that he has allowed his civilization to outdistance his culture.... mentality to outrun his morality. He has allowed his technology to outdistance his theology."

Echoing King's admonitions, DeYoung tells us his Biblical exhortations were inspired and "informed by places of activism" (in the quest for morality). They "invite racial justice action to be expressed in community (culture of relationships) and rooted in a direct, vibrant relationship with God (expressions of theology). So, "to stay woke" around issues of racial and economic justice is not a new conversation. Using the sacred texts to chronicle today's sites of resistance and revolution, DeYoung reminds us of the cost of following the Gospel of Jesus Christ and being an agent of God's activism.

Read this book if you need a pick me up, some "I ain't crazy" self-speak (ah hah), and a hopeful jolt as you seek to do Jesus' justice. Read this book if you need in-between time to rest, abide, pray, and heal in the Spirit from the wounds of being a warrior disciple. Read this book to

- Face the dissonance between human anger and Holy rage,
- Be a better resurrection witness,
- Learn to hear another's truths,
- Think more deeply about what Jesus's justice looks like,
- Have the courage to ask *can white Christianity free itself of white supremacy?*
- Confront our fears around reparations and radical reconciliation,
- Name what is required of us to end empire,
- Manage our disappointments and pain when co-disciples become spectators or, worse yet, betrayers of the movement,
- Acknowledge the need for lamentation,
- Grapple with the meaning of the Pentecost and God's intent around diversity, and
- Connect the responsibility for all of God's creation with our expression of our humanity.

No doubt, we have entered an age of the Metaverse, avatars, and artificial intelligence. Today's activists must engage the powerful media technologies and enterprises that can be dehumanizing and shape the behaviors of people and the outcomes of events. Add to that, increasing xenophobia, state-sanctioned violence, normalization of racialized hate speech, and a well-organized ultra-right. Remaining awake or staying woke requires attention to one's holistic consciousness of being.

For many who hover at the intersection of justice and faith, one of the greatest challenges they face is the challenge of self-care, not mere physical self-care, but mental, emotional, and spiritual self-care. DeYoung's sermonic reflections are so helpful and timely for today's activists. He connects enduring scriptures with the wisdom of the ages so that we might breathe, and our souls are protected from the assaults of what King warned against: fear, dangerous optimism, and technology without a theology.

With authority and authenticity, DeYoung's final word offers a powerful anecdote of hope for activists to embrace. This anecdote is grounded in the French creole name of God, *Bondyé bon*. This translates to "Goodgod is good!"

The Risk of Being Woke: Sermonic Reflections for Activists is a book to keep by the bedside or altar. With a hookup to the divine, it takes us back and moves us forward at the same time. We are forever charged to stay woke, being and knowing our "Goodgod is good."

Dr. Iva E. Carruthers
General Secretary
Samuel DeWitt Proctor Conference

Notes
1. Oberlin June 1965 commencement "Remaining Awake Through a Great Revolution."

Acknowledgments

This book reflects my return to full-time racial justice action through faith-based organizations in Chicago and Minneapolis after several years as a racial justice academic. I am grateful that Judson Press chose to publish these sermonic reflections. They published my first book in 1995, and now this is our fifth project together. These reflections had the benefit of some typing assistance as they were converted from handwritten notes. Thanks to Rachel DeYoung, Jonathan DeYoung, Julia Hobart, and Chrissie Carver. My family has called Park Avenue United Methodist Church in Minneapolis our home for many years. Several of these sermonic reflections were premiered in the pulpit of Park Avenue Church. I am grateful for a supportive and encouraging faith community.

Thank you to the staffs and boards of the Community Renewal Society (Chicago) and the Minnesota Council of Churches (Minneapolis) who provided places to serve that shaped the content of this book. I offer a special thanks for the profound influence of the Samuel DeWitt Proctor Conference—especially Iva E. Carruthers, Jeremiah A. Wright Jr., James A. Forbes, Jr., J. Alfred Smith, Traci Blackmon, Frederick Douglass Haynes III, Starsky Wilson, Gina M. Stewart, and Wendell L. Griffen. My understanding of racial justice has been refined and shaped through their tutelage and relationship.

During the immediate aftermath of the murder of George Floyd, I was contacted by folks who had gone through similar situations in other cities offering their personal support and encouragement. In particular, I want to thank Traci Blackmon, Waltrina N.

Middleton, Frank Madison Reid III, Jacqui Lewis, Osagyefo Sekou, and Timothy J. Clarke.

I am grateful for the ongoing support of my wife, Karen, and my children, Rachel, Jonathan, and Dane. There are many friends who have been in my corner, including Robin R. Bell, Aldean Miles, Cecilia Williams, Cheryl J. Sanders, Allan Aubrey Boesak, Stacey L. Smith, and Richard J. Howell, Jr. These past ten years have been costly in the deaths of several friends. Two of my most important mentors were among those deaths: James Earl Massey (2018) and Cain Hope Felder (2019). In so many ways this book reflects their contributions to my journey and to the importance of the sermonic in action, community, and mysticism.

There are many preaching mentors and colleagues who have shaped my own encounter with the intersection of Scripture and racial justice action. At this writing there is one who deserves special mention, my friend, the late Walstone Francis (died in 2020), former senior pastor at Shiloh Baptist Church in Waukegan, Illinois. In our organizing work together in Chicago and Waukegan, I had the pleasure of observing as my friend and co-conspirator for racial justice made protest preaching an art form.

With much gratitude to God!

Identifiers Used

Designating groups and people by race and culture is always a tentative task. This book uses terminology that reflects accepted usage at the time of writing: African American and Black; Native American and Indigenous; Asian; Latine; and white. I do not use the word Caucasian. This identifier for whites of European descent was used to designate whites as superior in a biological race hierarchy. Caucasoids were superior to Mongoloids who were superior or to Negroids by birth and genetic makeup. Since I reject the notion of biological race, I also reject the use of these terms. I use BIPOC (Black, Indigenous, People of Color) and the phrase "People of Color" when speaking collectively of people who are not white. These are imperfect terms. But when discussing historic injustices based on white racial superiority, a term that includes all who are not white is needed.

Introduction

Remaining Awake in a Racial Reckoning

The Risk of Being Woke: Sermonic Reflections for Activists is a twenty-first-century call to embrace racial justice action, live in beloved community, and seek refreshing mystic moments as we emerge from a health pandemic and engage in a racial reckoning. I live and write in the city of Minneapolis, the national epicenter of a racial reckoning, in the state of Minnesota, where some of the United States' worst racial disparities exist. My home and the church I attend are a few blocks from where George Floyd was killed on May 25, 2020. On the two-year anniversary, the area was officially renamed George Perry Floyd Square. I am the CEO of the Minnesota Council of Churches—an organization that has intentionally transformed its governance structure from one that de facto guaranteed white dominance to one where heads of Black denominations lead and the board of directors is comprised of a majority of Black, Indigenous, Latine, and Asian leaders. The council has launched a ten-year racial justice programmatic commitment to truth-telling, education, and reparations.

This book is a collection of deep reflections on racial justice and Scripture, most of which were shared first in the pulpit. The reflections have been expanded in written form to appeal to the eye as well as the ear. Yet, a sermonic feel has been retained. These biblical exhortations invite racial justice action to be expressed in community and rooted in a direct, vibrant relationship with God. This book is informed by places of activism. Each chapter centers on the biblical call for faith-inspired activists to work for justice and reminds online-focused believers that the need for in-person community still exists and encourages weary yet faithful people to find spiritual meaning in the season just survived.

The global COVID-19 health pandemic and the protests and unrest following the killing of George Floyd by law enforcement in Minneapolis, Minnesota, brought renewed public attention to historic racial disparities in the United States. The gaps in home ownership, wealth, educational outcomes, health, incarceration, employment, public safety, and other social indicators between whites and Black, Indigenous, and People of Color (BIPOC) communities reveal the entrenched effects of systemic racism. These long-term inequities created the growing tensions that resulted in uprisings across the United States in 2020.

Nowhere in the United States are these disparities starker than in the Twin Cities of Minnesota where I live. The Minneapolis/St. Paul metropolitan area is one of the best places in the United States for whites to live. Shortly after the death of George Floyd, then-NAACP President Leslie Redmond called the Twin Cities the "white Wakanda."[1] At the same time, it is one of the worst places for African Americans to live.[2] Longtime Minneapolis civil rights activist Spike Moss noted, "You were disrespected your entire life during Jim Crow, which is the reason my mother brought us to Minnesota. Turns out Minnesota is Mississippi up north."[3] Thus, the explosive outburst after the traumatic murder of George Floyd was not shocking to local activists and academics focused on racial dynamics. The conditions were ripe for such a moment.

As we awake from a multiyear pandemic, we are tempted to slumber through the injustices still facing us. We need to stay awake to the realities of our social order and work for racial justice. But we also need to be cognizant that there are risks involved in being awake or woke. This book reminds readers that the risks to physical safety, emotional stability, communal unity, and spiritual vitality are real. Yet for more than two thousand years, the power of God and the way of Jesus have enabled people of faith to persevere in the face of unjust systems and announce the good news of a faith-inspired alternate vision of a just society.

The title of this book comes from the sermonic reflection found in chapter 1. I was scheduled to preach on Palm Sunday in April 2020. I planned to use the text from the Gospel of John, which centers on the account of Jesus raising Lazarus from the dead in the Palm Sunday narrative. I consulted the relevant commentaries and constructed the manuscript. When the pandemic shelter-in-place orders came from health officials, the dynamics of preaching shifted to a virtual format and the scheduled preaching assignment did not occur. I did not preach virtually during this season of watching from home, feeling lost without a pulpit and people in the sanctuary.[4] A year later, when it came time for Palm Sunday 2021, I was invited to join a virtual discussion with Rev. Lina Thompson and Dr. Tali Hairston of Lake Burien Presbyterian Church in Seattle. Instead of traditional preaching, they were engaging in sermonic conversations. I reviewed my research notes from the Gospel of John sermon prep in 2020 and readied myself for the pre-taped Sunday dialogue. In that Palm Sunday conversation, I shared that the raising of Lazarus from the dead by Jesus brought a death sentence for Jesus . . . and for Lazarus! I noted the risks involved when you are aligned with Jesus. Lazarus was sentenced to death because Jesus woke him up (John 11:11).

At the end of the conversation, I was asked for a sermon title. Without giving it much thought, I blurted out, "The Risk of Being Woke." The opening chapter offers a more complete telling of the Lazarus and Jesus narrative embedded in the triumphal entry event and discusses in greater detail the history and complexities of the term "woke" in today's activist vernacular and the political pushback from various sectors of society. Briefly, "woke" was used as early as the 1930s in the African American community as a warning to stay alert in the face of racism. In 2014, Black Lives Matter activists used "woke" in reference to police shootings of Black people during the Ferguson protests. Currently, the word *woke* is used beyond the Black community with whites calling themselves woke as allies in matters of racism, while others use it to mock social justice activists.

The proposal for this book took shape during two weeks of solitude at the Gulf Shores in Alabama while reading Howard Thurman and pondering the contents of this volume. Daily walks on the beach and quiet contemplation replenished my soul and reignited my writing. As I organized this volume, I felt that it was necessary to consider an activist life rooted in community that intersects with a mystic mindset. Fifteen years ago, I published a book called *Living Faith: How Faith Inspires Social Justice,*[5] a study of faith-inspired activists I called mystic-activists. I borrowed this term from theologian Alton B. Pollard III, who had used this identifier to define Howard Thurman.[6] While Thurman was a mystic in the traditional sense of pursuing a deeply personal experience with the divine, he did not hide away in the inward journey. His mysticism propelled him to engage society, particularly in addressing racism.

A deeply spiritual life also enabled Thurman to survive the challenges of racism and gain a glimpse of a future that could be more just. Thurman wrote:

> I have sought a way of life that could come under the influence of, and be informed by, the fruits of the inner life. The cruel vicissitudes of the social situation in which I have been forced to live in American society have made it vital for me to seek resources, or a resource, to which I could have access as I sought means for sustaining the personal enterprise of my life beyond all of the ravages inflicted upon it by the brutalities of the social order. To live under

siege, with the equilibrium and tranquility of peace, to pre-
vent the springs of my being from being polluted by the
bitter fruit of the climate of violence, to hold and re-hold
the moral initiative of my own action and to seek the experience of community, all of this to whatever extent it has
been possible to achieve it, is to walk through a door that
no [one] can shut.[7]

I expanded Pollard's notion about Thurman as a mystic-activist
to also include activists who have or should have a mystic sensibil-
ity. Our activism needs to reach passionately inward toward the
divine for sustenance, wisdom, perseverance, and belonging. Our
outward activism needs inward mysticism. In their book *Oscar
Romero: Reflections of His Life and Writings*, authors Marie
Dennis, Renny Golden, and Scott Wright rightly note that activists
"who are caught in the fire of history and nudged by the great maw
of justice rarely court the inner realms of mysticism." As activists
for racial justice, we cannot "endure the scandal and scourge
[evoked] without an inner life of fathomless depth and intensity."[8]

The risks that come with being woke to racial justice activism
require a life fully engaged in committed community and a spirit
deeply rooted in a relationship with God. Therefore, these sermonic reflections for mystic-activists are meant to nurture and nudge us
as we encounter risks in the midst of the journey. This book is
divided into three sections that call us into the biblically inspired
work of racial justice through action, community, and mystic
moments. The work of the sermonic amid the call for racial justice
is a collective venture. While this book is not academic per se,
numerous citations acknowledge the earthly and heavenly cloud of
witnesses who contributed to or originated the sermonic insights
contained herein. The list of citations and the bibliography not only
hint at the sermonic process, but also should be considered as a rich
interpretive resources for the readers.

This book can be read from beginning to end. Yet each chapter is structured so it can be read on its own. This allows readers to selectively peruse by Scripture text, topic of interest, or the prompting of a current racial justice event or crisis. Also, the book chapters and section introductions can serve as devotional reflections. For preachers, teachers, and activists among the readers, I hope these reflections can serve as inspiration for your own oratorical callings.

Notes

1. Hannah Flood, "Minneapolis NAACP President: 'We All Have a Position, We All Have a Duty to Activate' in Confronting Racism," KMSP, June 28, 2020, www.fox9.com/news/minneapolis-naacp-president-we-all-have-a-position-we-all-have-a-duty-to-activate-in-confronting-racism. Wakanda is the name of the fictional idyllic nation brought into popular consciousness in the movie *Black Panther*.

2. Christopher Ingraham, "Racial Inequality in Minneapolis among the Worst in the Nation," *Washington Post*, May 30, 2020, https://www.washingtonpost.com/business/2020/05/30/minneapolis-racial-inequality/. See also Leslie Redmond and Curtiss Paul DeYoung, "White Privilege Shines with COVID-19," *StarTribune*, April 23, 2020, https://www.startribune.com/white-privilege-shines-with-covid-19/569903692/.

3. Spike Moss, quoted in Rohan Preston and Jenna Ross, "Seeking Justice, Leaving a Legacy," *StarTribune*, Autumn 2020, 29.

4. On January 16, 2022, I was scheduled to preach in person for the ordination of Daniel Romero at First Christian Church in Minneapolis. I tested positive for COVID the night prior to the service and finally had to deliver a sermon on Zoom.

5. Curtiss Paul DeYoung, *Living Faith: How Faith Inspires Social Justice* (Minneapolis: Fortress, 2007).

6. Alton B. Pollard III, *Mysticism and Social Change: The Social Witness of Howard Thurman* (New York: Peter Lang, 1992), 1, 62.

7. Howard Thurman, *Mysticism and the Experience of Love* (Wallingford, PA: Pendle Hill Pamphlet 115, 1961), 5.

8. Marie Dennis, Renny Golden, and Scott Wright, *Oscar Romero: Reflections on His Life and Writings* (Maryknoll, NY: Orbis Books, 2000), 19.

The Call to Action
The Power of the Prophet Never Dies

As a man was being buried, a marauding band was seen and the man was thrown into the grave of Elisha; as soon as the man touched the bones of Elisha, he came to life and stood on his feet. (2 Kings 13:21)

This obscure text from 2 Kings offers a unique and powerful metaphor for the call to action for racial justice. Elisha the prophet was dead and buried. He had been dead so long that only his bones remained in the grave. A few years after Elisha's death, a funeral was in process in the same cemetery where the late prophet was buried. The funeral was interrupted by bandits, and the man who was being eulogized was thrown into the closest random tomb. It so happened that the man's body landed in the grave of the prophet Elisha—one of the greatest prophets in the history of ancient Israel. As the dead man's body fell into the tomb, it brushed against the dry bones of the remains of Elisha. Immediately the man "came to life and stood on his feet." The bones of the dead prophet Elisha had greater power and vitality than any of the living kings still sitting on their thrones who had experienced the fervor of Elisha's prophetic words.

In our efforts at racial justice, we sometimes feel as though our prophetic work is dead. We speak truth to power with no visible victory. We embrace the prophetic call to action and then experience the death of our hopes and aspirations for justice. At the end of a season with few victories we lament. We funeralize our efforts at justice. We feel like death . . . a death of hoped-for outcomes . . . a death of just legislation . . . a death of righteous efforts.

This story from 2 Kings reminds us that the power of the prophet never dies. The text encourages us to touch the bones of our prophetic justice efforts. We must hold onto the racial justice we have worked so hard to achieve. By holding onto the calls for and acts of justice, we are touching the prophetic words that give us life. The text assures us that if we touch the bones we will come to life and we will stand on our feet . . . ready to fight for justice yet another day! God is a God of life—even life-giving dead bones.

While lament is necessary and even required, we cannot remain there. Have we buried our hopes and dreams? Have we let go of what should be and settled for what is? Let me remind you that we are also people who believe in a Jesus who said, "I am the resurrection and the life" (John 11:25). Our work is never in vain. The seeds of future justice have been planted. Martin Luther King Jr. would often quote from William Cullen Bryant, "Truth crushed to Earth will rise again."[1] What seems like the end is often just the prelude to a new beginning. Death can produce life. The power of the prophet never dies. We are a resurrection people!

This obscure text from the Hebrew Bible's narrative arc of the prophet Elisha reminds us that the power of prophetic pronouncements against racial injustice cannot be silenced. So, this first section is a call to twenty-first-century prophets of racial justice action. The chapters in section 1 remind us that the risk of activism goes hand in hand with the biblical call to address empire realities; the cry that Black Lives Matter is rooted in the biblical witness that all oppressed lives matter; and the Jesus of today never contradicts the

Jesus who preached good news to the poor in the first century. We also observe an exchange between a Greek woman and the colonized Jewish Jesus that suggests how conversations about racism can be framed; a strategy implemented by the apostle Paul that offers some insights into economic equity and reparations; and a narrative that reveals why ending empire is fraught with challenges. The final chapter in this section speaks to the place and practice of our calling.

Notes

1. Martin Luther King Jr., "If the Negro Wins, Labor Wins," in *A Testament of Hope: The Essential Writings and Speeches of Martin Luther King Jr.*, ed. James M. Washington (San Francisco: HarperSanFrancisco, 1986), 207.

CHAPTER 1

The Risk of Being Woke

Our friend Lazarus has fallen asleep; but I am going there
to wake him up. (John 11:11, NIV)

Meanwhile a large crowd of Jews found out that Jesus
was there and came, not only because of him but also to
see Lazarus, whom he had raised from the dead. So the
chief priests made plans to kill Lazarus as well, for on
account of him many of the Jews were going over to
Jesus and putting their faith in him. (John 12:9-11, NIV)

Martin Luther King Jr. preached what would be his final Sunday
sermon on March 31, 1968, at the National Cathedral in
Washington, DC. His sermon title was "Remaining Awake
through a Great Revolution."[1] He set the context for his sermon
by retelling Washington Irving's story of Rip Van Winkle. King
recounted how Rip Van Winkle had climbed up a mountain and
fell asleep for what would be twenty years. When he went up the
mountain, there was a sign that had a picture of King George III of
England. When he came down the mountain after sleeping for
twenty years, the sign had a picture of George Washington, the first
president of the United States. King noted that Rip Van Winkle had
slept through a revolution.

Martin Luther King was concerned that people were sleeping
through the revolution occurring in 1968. He said that day, "One

of the greatest liabilities of life is that all too many people find themselves living amid a great period of social change and yet they fail to develop the new attitudes, the new mental responses—that the new situation demands. They end up sleeping through a revolution."[2] The killing of George Floyd in Minneapolis in 2020 unleashed a great revolution and a global racial reckoning. We must remain awake! We cannot fall asleep. As King said in 1968, we must develop the new attitudes, the new mental responses, that the new situation demands. To do that, we must remain awake.

Today, the word *woke* is often used to succinctly situate the notion of remaining awake through a great revolution. The word *woke* dates back at least to the 1930s as a word used in African American community vernacular to warn folks to stay alert and vigilant in the face of ever-present racism. The first recorded use of *woke* was in a spoken afterword in an audiotape by blues musician Lead Belly in 1938 for a song entitled "Scottsboro Boys"—a song warning Blacks about racism in Alabama. After the song ends, Lead Belly warns the listeners that they "best stay woke, keep their eyes open."[3]

The word *woke* entered public and popular consciousness in 2014 when Black Lives Matter activists used it during the Ferguson protests in reference to police shootings of Black people. By 2016, it was declared a slang word of the year by the American Dialect Society. In 2017, it was included in the Oxford Dictionary.[4] Now, the word *woke* is used beyond the Black community and regarding issues other than racism. Some whites refer to themselves as woke to express their allyship in matters of racism. While well-intentioned, this usage carries the possibility of being perceived as cultural appropriation or at the least self-serving. Woke is even now used as an insult by those who seek to challenge and block efforts at racial justice. The *Daily Mail* newspaper in England said of the work of Prince Harry and Meghan that Prince Harry had changed from a "fun loving bloke to . . . Prince of Woke."[5]

Martin Luther King asked folks to remain awake in 1968. Black Lives Matter activists asked people to stay woke in 2014 as Ferguson, and many other places then, before, and since, experienced the killing of Black people by police. It was a great revolution, a resistance to state-sponsored killings, and an upswell of protest. With the uprising in 2020 in Minneapolis following the killing of George Floyd, we need to stay awake, stay woke, so we do not sleep through, and miss, what God is doing. It is time to leave the classroom of wokeness now that we have established the need to remain awake in this great revolution and the racial reckoning birthed in Minneapolis.

The text from the Gospel of John and the narrative and context in which it is embedded beckons us to consider the risk of being woke—that is, the risk of being awake. Chapters 11 and 12 in the Gospel of John bring together two central narratives: the raising of Lazarus from the dead by Jesus (11:1-54) and Jesus' triumphal entry into Jerusalem for the Passover (11:55–12:19). The story of the raising from the dead of Lazarus was not included in the synoptic Gospels—Matthew, Mark, and Luke. The synoptic Gospels are often considered to be based on the testimony of Jesus' disciple Peter, who disappears from John's narrative in chapters 7 through 12. While Peter was typically the spokesperson for the twelve disciples, in our text Thomas plays that role. Biblical scholar Leon Morris suggests that Peter may have remained in Galilee as Jesus and other disciples went to Bethany. Then he joined them in Jerusalem for Passover week.[6]

Passover was a hotbed of political intrigue and tension. Once a year two to three million Jews entered Jerusalem—much like the Islamic Hajj in Mecca today.[7] Passover was a ritualized retelling and celebration of Moses liberating the ancient Israelites from their Egyptian oppressors who had held them as slaves for generations. During the time of Jesus, Jews were colonized by the Roman Empire. They experienced the racism of a Roman

7

supremacist belief system that considered Jews were "a people born for servitude"[8] and "good for nothing but slavery."[9] As the liberation from Egyptian slaveholders was retold, you can imagine how easy it was to apply that to Rome and call for liberation from their current oppressors.

Jewish historian Josephus noted two Passover riots that occurred when the Roman military occupying Jerusalem flaunted their claimed supremacy. In the first case, the imperial forces in Jerusalem placed Roman eagle statues over the entrance to the temple. This was seen as a defilement of the holy, and a riot occurred. In a second case, a Roman soldier "bared his backside" to the Jewish people. Once again, a riot ensued. In both situations, thousands of worshippers were killed, and Rome canceled Passover during those years.[10] There was always much tension in Jerusalem as Passover approached.

The provincial governor Pilate always arrived prior to Passover with a sizable regiment of law enforcement and military to control any possible protest or unrest. This was "standard practice of the Roman governors of Judea to be in Jerusalem for the major Jewish festivals."[11] Biblical scholars Marcus Borg and John Dominic Crossan offer a glimpse of the sights and sounds of imperial power: "calvary on horses, foot soldiers, leather armor, helmets, weapons, banners, golden eagles mounted on poles, sun glinting on metal and gold [and] the marching of feet, the creaking of leather, the clinking of bridles, the beating of drums."[12]

Jesus stepped directly and intentionally into these tensions as he traveled from Galilee to Jerusalem and the Passover event. With his growing popularity among the oppressed and marginalized masses in Palestine, Jesus was considered a threat. The local political and religious leaders who were in league with Rome did all they could to ensure order. Beginning in John 7 and onward, we read of plans to kill Jesus. A network of informants kept Jesus under surveillance and reported to the Jerusalem leaders on his activities.

When Jesus declared that he was going to wake up Lazarus, his disciples expressed their fears and concerns. Jesus said, "Our friend Lazarus has fallen asleep; but I am going to wake him up" (11:11, NIV). Once the disciples understood that Jesus intended to raise Lazarus from the dead, Thomas said, "Let us also go, that we may die with him" (11:16, NIV). The disciples understood that raising Lazarus from the dead would be a further catalyst for killing Jesus. They did not question if Jesus could raise Lazarus, but rather if he would risk his own life to do it. Raising Lazarus set in motion a "chain of events that was to lead to his death."[13]

Jesus did indeed raise Lazarus from the dead back to life after he had been in the grave for four days.[14] The Jerusalem leaders were concerned for their own positions of power: "If we let him go on like this, everyone will believe in him, and then the Romans will come and take away both our place and our nation" (11:48, NIV). Jerusalem leaders were afraid that Jesus' growing popularity and increased number of followers could cost them their collaboration with the Roman Empire. The Sanhedrin immediately issued a warrant for Jesus' arrest, and the chief priest declared a death sentence. When the high priest issued a death sentence, his words could not be revoked.[15]

Jesus and his disciples went underground until the Passover. They hid in a town near the wilderness to avoid arrest. John wrote that Jesus "no longer moved about publicly" (11:54, NIV). A similar story comes from 1961. Nelson Mandela went into hiding to avoid arrest by the apartheid South African government. He continued to travel about the country, but in disguise "as a chauffeur, complete with the old fashioned dark blue coat with brass buttons, and a traditional chauffeur's cap."[16] Mandela was arrested in 1962 with information provided by the Central Intelligence Agency (CIA) of the United States.[17] Unlike Mandela, Jesus and his disciples were able to avoid arrest. The Roman Empire did not have the assistance of the CIA. On the eve of the Passover week, Jesus and his disciples re-emerged in Bethany at the home of Martha, Mary, and Lazarus.

In John 12, we learn that Lazarus was also sentenced to death. "The chief priests made plans to kill Lazarus as well, for on account of him many of the Jews were going over to Jesus and putting their faith in him" (12:10-11, NIV). All Lazarus did was wake up. He was sentenced to death for being woke. It was at this moment in my study of this narrative that I realized that there are risks to being woke (awake). Lazarus was at risk, sentenced to death because he was woke. Biblical scholar Otto Linn called Lazarus "a living monument" to the power of Jesus.[18] Lazarus was at risk because he was evidence that Jesus had the power to change circumstances from death to life.

The raising of Lazarus demonstrated that God's power was greater than that of Jerusalem and Rome. God's power was centered in the margins and in places of death. Lazarus was seen as a threat to the status quo because he was aligned with Jesus. Because of Lazarus, many were putting faith in Jesus. Lazarus was a key reason for the growth of a mass movement in Palestine. This can be observed in the Gospel of John. The author described three separate crowds merging into one mass multitude of people as they marched to Jerusalem. There was the crowd of Galileans who traveled with Jesus. There was the crowd from Bethany that had observed the raising of Lazarus. And a third crowd of folks gathered in Jerusalem for the Passover had heard about the raising of Lazarus by Jesus. They came out of the city toward Bethany to join the other two crowds.

Lazarus was already at risk as a colonized Jew and a marginalized person who came from a nontraditional family situation. He was an unmarried adult male living with his two unmarried adult sisters in a female head-of-household home. Jesus raised to life a marginalized Jew. Marginalized Jewish lives mattered. Lazarus was at risk not only due to his status as a colonized and marginalized person aligned with Jesus, but he was also put at greater risk as a woke activist.

We are at risk when we are awake, when we are woke, when we work for racial and social justice, and when we align ourselves with Jesus. We are at risk when we pose a threat to the status quo by disrupting the myth of white supremacy. We are at risk when we challenge the empire, because the empire will strike back. We are at risk from informants who will betray us. We are at risk from the power of injustice itself. There is a risk to being woke, to being awake. Being awake through a great revolution and a racial reckoning bears risk. There is a risk of being woke in the struggle for racial justice and equity.

As I reflected on the story of Lazarus, an insight emerged. I discovered an answer to the quandary of the risks faced when one has been woken up by Jesus. The political leaders of Jerusalem placed a death sentence on Lazarus. They placed a death sentence on someone who had already died and been raised from the dead by Jesus. The logic of faith says that if Jesus had raised Lazarus from the dead, he was capable of doing it again. The empire would not and could not have the final word. The logic of faith says to us today that if Jesus has woke us up and called us, then Jesus will sustain us and empower us when folks try to kill our commitment, when the naysayers challenge our sincerity or intellect, or even when racial justice work itself becomes exhausting and overwhelming. The dead bones of prophetic justice still contain life-giving power. Where there is death, Jesus breathes life. Where there is risk, Jesus offers holy resolve. So, let us remain awake through this great revolution by putting our trust in Jesus, who is the way, the truth, and the life.

Notes

1. Martin Luther King Jr., "Remaining Awake through a Great Revolution," in *A Testament of Hope: The Essential Writings and Speeches of Martin Luther King*

Jr., ed. James M. Washington (San Francisco: HarperSanFrancisco, 1986), 268–78.

2. Ibid., 269.

3. Aja Romano, "A History of Wokeness," *Vox*, October 29, 2020, www.vox.com/culture/21437879/stay-woke-wokeness-history-origin-evolution-controversy. See also Lead Belly, "Scottsboro Boys," from *Lead Belly: The Smithsonian Folkways Collection* (2015); to listen to the recording: www.youtube.com/watch?v=VrXfkPViFIE&t=4s.

4. Katy Steinmetz, "The Oxford English Dictionary Just Added 'Woke.' It's Older Than You Think," *Time*, June 25, 2017, www.time.com/4830959/oxford-english-dictionary-woke/.

5. "Once Prince Harry Was the Life and Soul of the Party, So How Did He Go from a Fun-Loving Bloke to . . . Prince of Woke?", *Daily Mail*, January 8, 2020, www.dailymail.co.uk/news/article-7866757/Prince-Harry-went-fun-loving-bloke-Prince-Woke.html.

6. Leon Morris, *The Gospel According to John* (Grand Rapids, MI: Eerdmans, 1971), 532–36.

7. Marianne Meye Thompson, *John: A Commentary* (Louisville, KY: Westminster John Knox, 2015), 263.

8. Neil Elliot, "The Apostle Paul and Empire," in *In the Shadow of Empire: Reclaiming the Bible as a History of Faithful Resistance*, ed. Richard A. Horsley (Louisville, KY: Westminster John Knox, 2008), 102.

9. Richard A. Horsley, *Jesus and Empire: The Kingdom of God and the New World Disorder* (Minneapolis: Fortress, 2003), 21. For the possibility that Jesus may have been born of a slave woman (his mother, Mary) and therefore been a slave himself (Philippians 2:7), see Mitzi J. Smith, "Abolitionist Messiah: A Man Named Jesus Born of a Doule," in *Bitter the Chastening Rod: Africana Biblical Interpretation After Stony the Road We Trod in the Age of BLM, SayHerName, and MeToo*, ed. Mitzi J. Smith, Angela N. Parker, and Ericka S. Dunbar Hill (Lanham, MD: Lexington Books/Fortress Academic, 2022), 53–70.

10. Thompson, 264.

11. Marcus J. Borg and John Dominic Crossan, *The Last Week: A Day-by-Day Account of Jesus's Final Week in Jerusalem* (San Francisco: HarperSanFrancisco, 2006), 2.

12. Ibid., 3.

13. Morris, *John*, 532.

14. Four days meant dead beyond resuscitation. See Gail R. O'Day, "The Gospel of John," in *The New Interpreter's Bible* vol. 9, ed. Leander E. Keck (Nashville: Abingdon, 1995), 687.

15. Bruce J. Malina and Richard L. Rohrbaugh, *Social Science Commentary on the Gospel of John* (Minneapolis: Fortress, 1998), 202.

16. Tony Hall, "Tony Hall's Interview with Nelson Mandela in Hiding," *Ars Notoria*, September 10, 2020, www.arsnotoria.com/2020/09/10/tony-halls-inter-view-with-nelson-mandela-in-hiding.

17. Ivan Fallon, "CIA Admits: We Sent Mandela to Jail," *The Sunday Times* (UK), May 15, 2016, www.thetimes.co.uk/article/cia-tip-off-led-to-jailing-of-mandela-9mwcsdq9c.

18. Otto F. Linn, *The Gospel of John* (Anderson, IN: Gospel Trumpet Company, 1942), 100.

CHAPTER 2

Oppressed Lives Matter

The Word became flesh and lived among us. (John 1:14)

Pilate also had an inscription written and put on the cross. It read, "Jesus of Nazareth, the King of the Jews." Many of the Jews read this inscription, because the place where Jesus was crucified was near the city, and it was written in Hebrew [Aramaic], in Latin, and in Greek. (John 19:19-20)

It was before your eyes that Jesus Christ was publicly exhibited as crucified! (Galatians 3:1)

God Taking on Humanity

Born in Bethlehem, raised in Nazareth of Galilee, and traversing the seldom-used paths of Samaria and the busy urban streets of Jerusalem, according to the Gospel of John, God "became flesh and lived among us" as Jesus of Nazareth (1:14). The *First Nations Version: An Indigenous Translation of the New Testament* states that God "became a flesh-and-blood human being and pitched his sacred tent among us, living as one of us."[1] Theologian Miguel De La Torre invites us to consider "which flesh was chosen for the incarnation. It was not Rome, the most powerful city of the known world . . . nor was it Jerusalem, the center of Yahweh worship;

rather it was impoverished Galilee."² The Gospel writer claimed that God did not join the human family as a prosperous person of privilege, power, and political connections, but rather lived among us as a Palestinian Jew from Galilee named Jesus. In other words, John declared that when God decided to visit planet Earth, the Divine took on the flesh of a colonized, oppressed, marginalized Jew living under the occupation of the first-century Roman Empire.

In the first century, the Roman Empire was one of the most hostile places for Jews to live. The lives of Jewish people were shaped by the daily realities of military occupation and political domination. Jesus experienced the stress of prejudice, the fear of Roman law enforcement, and the ever-present reality of being crucified or lynched. John began his Gospel with the stunning claim that God took on flesh as a Palestinian Jew. Early fifth-century African church leader Augustine wrote in his *Confessions*, "he was counted as one of our number, and he paid his dues to Caesar."³

At the Site of Crucifixion

I visited Ferguson, Missouri, with other faith leaders in 2014. I was deeply moved as we spent time in reflection at the place where Michael Brown was killed by law enforcement and lay dead in the street for four and a half hours. This was the very place where his mother held vigil near his dead body as it lay in the street exposed and unattended for those four and a half hours. This lack of care and concern by Ferguson city leaders for the body of Michael Brown is emblematic of a historic disregard for the lives of Black people in the United States. This is why the refrain "Black Lives Matter" echoes across the nation.

As I have noted, when the Gospel writer spoke of God taking on human flesh, it is important to remember that Jesus was a first-century Jew, a colonized and oppressed person. In the first century, the

Roman Empire held an extreme disregard for Jewish people, like Black people in the twenty-first-century United States. Crucifixions of Jews were the ultimate symbol of this historic disregard—"paying dues to Caesar." After Jesus died, he remained hanging on a cross for about four and a half hours. His mother, Mary, held a vigil of grief for her son at the site of his crucifixion.

As a matter of course, Jews were executed because their lives did not matter. The Roman Empire used crucifixion to terrorize their Jewish subjects. Biblical scholar Richard A. Horsley writes, "As with other forms of terrorism, crucifixions were displayed in prominent places for the 'demonstration effect' on the rest of the population . . . Seeing their relatives, friends, and other fellow villagers suffering such agonizing death would presumably intimidate the surviving populace into acquiescence in the reestablished Roman imperial order."[4] The apostle Paul referred to the public nature and state terror intention of Jesus' crucifixion when he wrote, "It was before your eyes that Jesus Christ was publicly exhibited as crucified!" (Galatians 3:1).

Crowds "gathered there for this spectacle" (Luke 23:48), as they regularly did, to watch the occurrence of crucifixion as a terrible sort of entertainment. Jesus was executed on a cross by Roman Empire law enforcement. Governor Pilate had it written "the King of the Jews"—an act of state-sponsored public racism, with signs declaring this in Aramaic, Greek, and Latin (John 19:19-20). For the Roman government, Jesus' crucifixion was representative of all Jews. Jewish lives were disposable and not valued in the Roman Empire. The three languages were used to communicate the Roman government's disdain for Jewish lives to all the society. Aramaic was the vernacular of Palestinian Jews. Greek was the language of the business community. Latin was the official language of the Roman Empire and its military. The use of the three languages also ensured that all Jews from the diaspora who were in Jerusalem for Passover were affronted by imperial condemnation.

Jesus was "a Jewish martyr of the Roman regime."[5] The lynching of thousands of Blacks in the history of the United States, similar in its purpose and scale to first-century crucifixions of Jews, was meant to terrorize Blacks and enforce their subjugation.[6] Lynching in the United States was advertised in newspapers and attracted large crowds of families with small children and smiling faces. Sometimes lynchings occurred directly after the Sunday morning services of white churches. Photos of lynchings were distributed as postcards and collectibles. It was so central to the nation's identity that writer and humorist Mark Twain coined the phrase, "The United States of Lyncherdom."[7]

Mary of Nazareth and Lezley McSpadden-Head (Michael Brown's mother) each held vigil for four and a half hours at the site of their sons' crucifixion. They witnessed the state's lack of regard for the lives of first-century Jews and twenty-first-century Blacks.

Resurrection Witness

Crucifixions demand resurrections. Three days later, this son of Mary who was killed by the Roman Empire as "the King of the Jews" was resurrected by God. Jesus was raised to life by God in response to the empire's act of death. The resurrection transformed Rome's public and systemic disregard into an action where God declared, "Jewish lives matter." The resurrection was God's response that Jewish lives matter, oppressed lives matter, Black Lives Matter. The resurrection of a Jew named Jesus reminded first-century Romans that no one could say all lives matter until Jewish lives were as important to society as they were to God.

Where is the resurrection hope in Ferguson for Michael Brown's mother? Where is the resurrection hope following the killings of Rekia Boyd and Laquan McDonald in Chicago, Breonna Taylor in Louisville, George Floyd and Amir Locke in Minneapolis, and so many more? Jesus' death was a state-sanctioned murder. God stepped in with resurrection, declaring Jewish lives mattered. What is the resurrection witness in the United States that declares that Black Lives Matter?

A significant disconnect exists between the experience and interpretation of Blacks and that of whites when it comes to racism in the United States. As the father of an African American son, the happenings in Ferguson, Missouri, created personal anxiety. I reflected at the time in an op-ed in the *Chicago Tribune*.[8] I noted that my lenses for interpretation included that I am an alumnus of Howard University (an HBCU) in Washington, DC, a current executive director of a historic civil rights organization in Chicago, and a racial justice scholar. Being the father of a Black son combined with these other identifiers created lenses through which I interpreted and experienced the pain and fear produced by Michael Brown's killing by police in Ferguson.

I was further transparent in admitting that "I am a white man, raised in a middle-class white suburb, with no personal experience of racism." My son and the dean at Howard University perceive policing through their direct experience of racism, as well as the narrative of a troubling history of racialized policing in Black communities. I continued, "If a police officer beckons to me, I never think that the color of my skin is the reason—that my life might be in danger."

Having lived in both white and Black worlds, I have seen the huge gap in lived experience that leads to radically different worldviews on issues of race. If resurrection calls for the viewpoint that Black Lives Matter, we must reconcile these opposed perceptions and beliefs. Generally, Blacks, Native Americans, Latine, and Asians have a necessary understanding of white viewpoints because they live their lives in and among the dominant white culture in the United States. Yet too many whites have no significant relationships with Persons of Color. A survey by the Public Religion Research Institute discovered that 75 percent of whites in the United States have no friends who are Persons of Color.[9] In other words, most whites have no conversations about racism and public safety with the persons most directly affected by racism and racialized policing. Ignorance is breeding more ignorance. This leads to a polarization of views that produces a lack of compassion, which leads to further psychic harm to people directly affected and affronted by racism. Whites must pause, listen, and consider the viewpoints of persons directly affected by racism. Greater awareness also comes through studying the history of racism in the United States. This increased awareness must prompt more racial justice action.

In the *Chicago Tribune* reflection, I referred to New York City hip-hop musician MADic, who critiques racialized policing and other social ills in his song "AmeriKKKa."[10] While he hopes for a more just society, he raps that until that happens, we must hang the flag upside down.[11] Until racial justice in policing comes to Ferguson, Chicago, Minneapolis, and the rest of the United States, we must hang the flag upside down. Hip-hop artist MADic is my son. He is Black. And he deserves justice in public safety. Until his life matters, I hang the flag upside down.

God took on flesh, was killed, and then resurrected. So, Jewish lives mattered, oppressed lives matter, Black Lives Matter. Word spread from one Jewish neighborhood to the next across Palestine, throughout the Roman Empire, and onto the continent of Africa that "Jewish lives matter." The same God who took on human flesh in Jesus to declare that Jewish lives matter is calling out to us today: Black Lives Matter, Indigenous lives matter, Asian lives matter, Brown lives matter, LGBTQ+ lives matter, Palestinian lives matter. The lives of people with disabilities are important. The lives of seniors have value. The lives of children matter. The lives of people working for inadequate wages and living in substandard housing are important. The lives of people being trafficked have value. The lives of unhoused and homeless people matter.

Someday, I hope, all lives will matter as much to us as they are valued by God.

Notes

1. *First Nations Version: An Indigenous Translation of the New Testament* (Downers Grove, IL: InterVarsity Press, 2021), 164.

2. Miguel A. De La Torre, *The Politics of Jesús: A Hispanic Political Theology* (Lanham, MD: Rowman & Littlefield, 2015), 81.

3. Augustine, *Confessions*, 5.3, in Marianne Meye Thompson, *John: A Commentary* (Louisville, KY: Westminster John Knox, 2015), 32.

4. Richard A. Horsley, *Jesus and Empire: The Kingdom of God and the New World Disorder* (Minneapolis: Fortress, 2003), 28.

5. Mark D. Nandos, *The Irony of Galatians: Paul's Letter in First-Century Context* (Minneapolis: Fortress, 2002), 205.

6. Equal Justice Initiative, *Lynching in America: Confronting the Legacy of Racial Terror* (Montgomery, AL: Equal Justice Initiative, 2017).

7. Mark Twain, "The United States of Lyncherdom," *Prospects* 25 (October 2000), 139–50, www.cambridge.org/core/journals/prospects/article/abs/ii-the-united-states-of-lyncherdom/2C02B2760694DA93C97CCBDFFEAB49F3.

8. Curtiss Paul DeYoung, "Race and Policing in America," *Chicago Tribune*, November 24, 2014, www.chicagotribune.com/opinion/commentary/ct-ferguson-police-michael-brown-darren-wilson-black-men-whites-perspec-1125-20141125-story.html.

9. Christopher Ingraham, "Three Quarters of Whites Don't Have Any Non-White Friends," *Washington Post*, August 25, 2014, www.washingtonpost.com/news/wonk/wp/2014/08/25/three-quarters-of-whites-dont-have-any-non-white-friends/.

10. MADic (Jonathan DeYoung), "AmeriKKKa," MADic EP, 2014.

11. The United States flag is typically hung upside down only as a signal of extreme distress and danger, like a call for help. Hanging the flag upside down has also become a way to protest issues with the government. It is not considered a desecration and is seen as an exercise of the First Amendment right. But it is not encouraged.

CHAPTER 3

The Same Jesus

Jesus Christ is the same yesterday and today and forever.
(Hebrews 13:8)

In the previous chapter, we took note of the implications of the claim made by the Gospel writer John that God entered history and "the Word became flesh" (John 1:14). The apostle Paul speaks of this same moment in time as "assuming human likeness . . . and being found in appearance as a human" (Philippians 2:7). According to the apostles John and Paul, God took on culture, race, gender identity, ethnicity, socioeconomic status, sexual orientation, and the like. The writer of Hebrews names this same season of history in reference to Jesus of Nazareth as "yesterday." What can we know about the person and life of yesterday's Jesus—the one claimed to be God made in human likeness, the Word become flesh?

Yesterday

Jesus' life began with the dramatic events surrounding his arrival: birth under scandalous circumstances, visits by poor shepherds from Palestine and Magi from Asia, and nighttime travel to the continent of Africa to find refuge from Herod's threats of murder. Jesus was born into an extended family with strong women— Elizabeth and Mary—and strong men—Zechariah and Joseph.

Jesus was born a descendant of the Hebrew people. Hebrew heritage found its roots in Asia, Africa, and the Indigenous people of Palestine. The family tree of Jesus was no different. It was multicultural and multiracial. Some scholars have called Jesus an Afro-Asiatic Jew.[1] Jesus had at least one drop of African blood running through his veins. According to the one-drop rule in the United States, he would be considered Black. That was yesterday's Jesus!

Jesus grew up in Galilee—the most culturally diverse province in first-century Palestine. In addition to Jews, Galilee included people from Assyria, Babylonia, Egypt, Macedonia, Persia, Rome, and Syria. Using today's language, Jesus grew up with Asians, Europeans, and Africans living nearby. Jesus spoke multiple languages. As a Galilean Jew, he spoke Aramaic in his house and in the streets, and he spoke Hebrew in the temple and synagogue. Working in his father's business, he also needed to speak Greek. As a subject of the Roman Empire, he might have spoken some Latin. That was yesterday's Jesus!

Jesus arrived on earth knowing all the power and privilege of divinity. Yet he let go of all that implied and took on human flesh as a poor, oppressed, first-century Jew under the domination and occupation of colonial Rome. That was yesterday's Jesus!

Jesus taught about the inclusive nature of the gospel: through parables, "Then people will come from east and west, from north and south, and take their places at the banquet in the kingdom of God" (Luke 13:29); through sermons, "My house shall be called a house of prayer for all the nations" (Mark 11:17); and through his daily life as he reached out in friendship and solidarity with women who traveled in his entourage (and raised funds for his ministry) and people outside of his cultural background. That was yesterday's Jesus!

Jesus died on a cross so that we might be reconciled to God and each other. An African, Simon of Cyrene, carried the cross, and a

European, a Roman centurion, spoke words of faith at the cross. Jesus was buried in a borrowed grave that was sealed and surrounded by all the power of the Roman Empire. On the third day, women disciples discovered that the grave was empty. Soon all his disciples heard a resurrected Jesus telling them to be his witnesses in Jerusalem, Judea, Samaria, and to the ends of the earth. That was yesterday's Jesus!

The resurrection released the Spirit of yesterday's Jesus, and it was evident in the life of the first-century church. What I have just said about Jesus could be seen in the church of the first century— from Jerusalem to Antioch, from Ephesus to Rome. The first-century church was made up of Jews, Samaritans, Greeks, Africans, Asians, Romans, and many others. The first-century church empowered women into leadership. The first-century church was repairing the breach between the powerless and the powerful, the poor and the rich, the marginalized and the privileged. The DNA of yesterday's Jesus was in the first-century church.

Sometime after yesterday and before today . . . the story of Jesus as an oppressed ethnic and religious minority person under the colonial rule of Rome was co-opted. The story of Jesus in solidarity with folks who were marginalized and as an activist for social justice was reconfigured. The story of Jesus as from a multiracial heritage and raised in a multicultural neighborhood was reissued. It was as though a virus was set loose and corrupted the reconciliation hard drive of the church. It was as though the DNA of yesterday's Jesus mutated into a form that Jesus himself would not recognize. The story of yesterday's Jesus was so radically altered that people across the modern era who were slave masters, dictators, crusaders, colonizers, white nationalists, homophobic, racist, sexist—even terrorists like the Ku Klux Klan—could claim to be Christians, followers of Jesus. I must remind you that it was not Jesus who changed. Jesus is the same yesterday and today and forever.

Today

So much more could be said about the Jesus of yesterday. Our text tells us that this same Jesus Christ of yesterday is here today. Jesus Christ is the same yesterday and today. Today's Jesus never contradicts yesterday's Jesus because Jesus Christ is the same yesterday, today, and forever. We can check today's claims about Jesus Christ against yesterday's Jesus in the Bible.

European colonizing forces arrived in the Americas armed with the papal doctrine of discovery claiming that Jesus called them to evangelize the world through the dispossession of land, eradication of culture, and the genocide of Indigenous people. A few Native people and a handful of whites looked to the Jesus of the Bible and discovered that the Jesus of the doctrine of discovery and manifest destiny was not the same Jesus as the Jesus in the Bible.

Slave traders sailed ships that were named "Jesus Saves," and slave masters said that their white Jesus endorsed the idea of Blacks being slaves. People of African descent wearing chains and some justice-minded whites looked to the Jesus of the Bible and discovered that the Jesus of the slave trader and slave master was not the same Jesus as the Jesus in the Bible.

Adolf Hitler seduced the Christian church in Germany to embrace a Nazi interpretation of Jesus and support the Shoah (holocaust of the Jews). Dietrich Bonhoeffer and a few others looked to the Jesus of the Bible and discovered that the Nazis' Jesus was not the same Jesus as the Jewish Jesus in the Bible.

White supremacists in the United States and South Africa claimed to be following Jesus. Fannie Lou Hamer and Martin Luther King, Desmond Tutu and Allan Boesak, and a host of others looked to the Jesus of the Bible and discovered that the Jesus of white supremacy was not the same Jesus as the Jesus in the Bible.

Even today, we can see Jesus presented as blessing materialism and cursing poverty and as presiding over the perks and privileges of corporate boardrooms. Jesus is even represented as though he was a citizen of the United States. When we look to the Jesus of the Bible, we discover that the privileged, patriotic Jesus of materialism, exceptionalism, and nationalism is not the same Jesus as the Jesus in the Bible. You do not need a PhD in theology to see that a lot of folks are creating a Jesus that serves their own agenda. As preacher Fred Craddock states, "The eternal sameness of Jesus Christ is the place to stand when the congregation is called on to deal with 'all kinds of strange teachings.'"[2]

Today's Jesus will never contradict yesterday's Jesus. Today's Jesus is found hanging out in the same kind of places and working on the same kind of issues as yesterday's Jesus. Jesus Christ is the same yesterday and today and forever.

Early in my ministry, I lived and worked in the Times Square region of New York City with the Covenant Faith Community, a group of Christians who committed themselves to prayer, community, simplicity, and service. At that time, Times Square was the center of sex trafficking in the United States. During the Christmas season, a number of us decided to go Christmas caroling in our neighborhood. I must admit that I had never experienced Christmas caroling like this. Our first stop was the Port Authority bus station. As we sang, we were joined by people who were living on the streets or were victims of the predatory sex industry in the area. Many presumably returned to life on the streets, but perhaps we planted a small seed of hope that eventually blossomed into a better life.

Our next stop was an adult sex shop. No one joined us as we sang, "round yon virgin mother and child."[3] The men who came and went either expressed anger or dropped their heads in shame and embarrassment. Many of them probably returned to pornographic bookstores in subsequent days, but perhaps someone remembered his wife and children at home and decided to honor his vow of faithfulness. While I have no idea what happened to the people who heard us sing, I want to believe that for someone in Times

Square, their evening was transformed into a silent night and a holy night. Christmas caroling in the bright lights of Times Square was a symbolic gesture that reminded us of where Jesus would hang out.

Even more so as activists, the issues Jesus cared about yesterday are the same issues we must care about today. We advocate for refugees and immigrants today because yesterday's Jesus was a refugee. We challenge Islamophobia today because yesterday's Jesus experienced the bigotry and hate faced by religious minorities. We address climate issues, gun violence, affordable housing, racism, sexism, and the like today because yesterday's Jesus had a full social justice ministry agenda. Because Jesus Christ is the same yesterday and today and forever, we can trust that today's Jesus never contradicts yesterday's Jesus, and we feel called today to hang out in the same places and work on the same issues as yesterday's Jesus.

Forever

Jesus Christ is the same yesterday and today and forever. The English translation obscures the actual word order in the Greek text, which would say, "Jesus Christ yesterday and today the same and forever."[4] This original order places due attention on "forever." The author of Hebrews claimed that there was a foreverness about Jesus Christ who will still be alive in "the time beyond the end of all days."[5] Jesus Christ transcended time.

This timeless foreverness of Jesus Christ declared by the author of Hebrews also causes us to think about our faith in ways that are beyond linear time. Illustrating this notion, theologian Randy Woodley reminds us that for Native Americans "there is a relationship between the present and the future . . . what we do today will impact the next seven generations [and] our past is forever in the present."[6] In Revelation, Jesus Christ is the alpha and the omega and is called the "root and the descendant of David" (22:16). As the root of David, Jesus is the source of David's whole family line.

26

He is also a descendant of David. It is impossible to be both the ancestor and the descendant of the same person, but Jesus Christ transcends time. I like the way Baptist preacher Manuel Scott Sr. proclaimed it: "Jesus was the only baby born older than his earthly mother and earthly father and just as old as his heavenly father."[7]

As biblical scholar James Earl Massey has preached, "Time poses no problem to his being nor his mission. . . . Time has not changed the person he is nor the position he holds."[8] To consider the foreverness of Jesus Christ claimed by the author of Hebrews means that we have a future-oriented approach to our racial justice action. Yes, our calling is rooted in the example of Jesus of Nazareth and our current activism and beliefs. Yet with a guiding sense of a Jesus who is the same forever, we can maintain a steady and informed hope. Our hope is sustained by an assured presence and an anticipated vision. Jesus Christ is the same yesterday and today and forever.

Notes

1. Cain Hope Felder, *Troubling Biblical Waters: Race, Class, and Family* (Maryknoll, NY: Orbis Books, 1989), 37; Curtiss Paul DeYoung, *Coming Together in the Twenty-First Century: The Bible's Message in an Age of Diversity* (Valley Forge, PA: Judson Press, 2009), 53–54.

2. Fred B. Craddock, "The Letter to the Hebrews," in *The New Interpreter's Bible* 12, ed. Leander E. Keck (Nashville: Abingdon, 1998), 165. "All kinds of strange teachings" is from Hebrews 13:9.

3. From "Silent Night, Holy Night (Stille Nacht, heilige Nacht)," lyrics by Joseph Mohr in 1816 and music by Franz Xaver Gruber in 1818.

4. William L. Lane, *Hebrews 9–13*, Word Biblical Commentary 47B (Nashville: Thomas Nelson, 1991), 522, 529.

5. *First Nations Version: An Indigenous Translation of the New Testament* (Downers Grove, IL: InterVarsity Press, 2021), 414.

6. Randy S. Woodley, *Shalom and the Community of Creation: An Indigenous Vision* (Grand Rapids, MI: Eerdmans, 2012), 119.

7. Manuel Scott, "He Is Alive," Billy Graham School of Evangelism (Asheville, NC), May 1988, audiocassette.

8. James Earl Massey, *Preaching from Hebrews: Hermeneutical Insights and Homiletical Helps* (Anderson, IN: Warner Press, 2014), 200. From "This Jesus," preached on Easter Sunday 1995 in Rankin Chapel at Howard University.

CHAPTER 4

Discussing Race in Dominant Spaces

Jesus left that place and went to the vicinity of Tyre. He entered a house and did not want anyone to know it; yet he could not keep his presence secret. In fact, as soon as she heard about him, a woman whose little daughter was possessed by an evil spirit came and fell at his feet. The woman was a Greek, born in Syrian Phoenicia. She begged Jesus to drive the demon out of her daughter.

"First let the children eat all they want," he told her, "for it is not right to take the children's bread and toss it to their dogs."

"Yes, Lord," she replied, "but even the dogs under the table eat the children's crumbs."

Then he told her, "For such a reply, you may go; the demon has left your daughter."

She went home and found her child lying on the bed, and the demon gone. (Mark 7:24-30, NIV)

The Context

Jesus left Galilee and traveled west to the city of Tyre—today in Lebanon. Tyre was a coastal city on the Mediterranean Sea. Jesus was looking for rest and quiet. He was overwhelmed by the crowds and stressed by the political pressures of King Herod and the Pharisees. Jesus entered a home. I like to think of it as a beach house retreat on the Mediterranean. This was probably the home of one of the few Jews living in Tyre.[1] As a Palestinian Jew, Jesus lived under the occupation and colonial rule of the Roman Empire. Growing up in Nazareth, people in his hometown experienced heavy taxation, house demolitions, and killings by Roman law enforcement.[2] Jesus would see thousands of crosses lining the highways when he went to Judea. Crucifixion was state-sponsored terrorism meant to intimidate Rome's Jewish subjects—similar to lynching in the history of the United States.

Jesus had been building a community of oppressed Jewish folks through a healing and teaching ministry, but he was tired. So, he left the occupied Jewish territories and ventured into the Greek city of Tyre—a place fully Gentile and elite. Word of Jesus' presence in this Greek city somehow got out. Because Jesus' healing ministry had included Greeks who came into the Jewish region of Galilee, he was known outside of his home. Even folks from Tyre had come into Galilee to see, hear, and be healed by Jesus.

Jesus was now in a space where the rules of dominant Greek culture operated. He was outside of his home territory and vulnerable as an oppressed Palestinian Jew. To use today's language, he was a BIPOC in a white privileged space—he had crossed into the white suburbs. In Tyre, Jesus stepped into a space where he must deal with racism and folks who believed in Roman Empire bigotry and stereotypes. Also, he must speak Greek, the language of the dominant culture, rather than his indigenous Aramaic.

The Conversation

A Greek woman from Syrian Phoenicia, where Tyre was located, walked into the house where Jesus was staying.[3] A conversation ensued between a racially oppressed person from a religious minority and a person enjoying the privileges provided by a Roman supremacist context. The conversation began when this Greek woman barged into the house and disrupted the rest and quiet of Jesus. She fell at his feet and begged Jesus to drive a demon out of her daughter. The woman was intently focused on her child. From her perspective, this was not an interruption of Jesus' rest or a disruption of cultural protocol. She was pleading for help.

Jesus replied, "First let the children eat all they want. For it is not right to take the children's bread and toss it to their dogs." Readers may be "horrified" to hear a gender slur coming from the lips of Jesus.[4] But "dog" was not a gender slur, as it is in our day.[5] Unfortunately, the meaning of the day was not any better. Rather, Jesus used a racial slur for Greeks by referring to them as "dogs." In first-century Jewish society, dogs were considered unclean. They ate scraps of food found on the streets. Sometimes they even ate the flesh off the corpses of homeless people who had died. In other words, Jesus was saying that his ministry was with oppressed Jews. He rejected her request because she was not Jewish.

Clearly, this text is controversial and challenging for biblical scholars. Some have pointed out that the Greek word translated as "dogs" is diminutive and should be understood as "puppies." Even then, a softer racial slur is still a racial slur. Perhaps Jesus had acquired certain prejudices from his socialization in first-century Jewish society under Roman domination. Therefore, he was expressing sentiments he had heard in his community of origin.

Here is what I think was happening: Jesus did not depart from or diminish his Jewish identity while in a Greek space. Jesus challenged her sensibilities, her parochialism, and her privilege. Could she understand what is needed to liberate oppressed people? When we sit in an airplane preparing for a commercial flight, we are told by the flight attendant that in case of emergency, we must put our own oxygen masks on first before we can help someone else. Jesus was saying that he had to first rescue oppressed Jews. First to the oppressed! First to Jews! Jewish Lives Matter! Jesus spoke his truth to the Greek woman from Syrian Phoenicia using strong racial terms. Perhaps he was testing her.[6]

The woman's response was, "Yes, Lord, but even the dogs under the table eat the children's crumbs." She persisted! She did not leave the conversation, nor did she get defensive. She did not personalize Jesus' comments. She spoke respectfully ("Lord") and did not argue with Jesus. Rather, she accepted that he was right; that he spoke truth; that Jews must be his priority. She did not argue that as a person of privilege she deserved his attention—or that he was being unfair. She did not argue that he should make an exception for her because she was not like other Greeks. She said in essence, while the oppressed must be your priority, we Greeks also need liberation and healing. We also need your help. Even those benefiting from systems of oppression need reconciliation.

The late Senator Robert Kennedy campaigned for the Democratic nomination for president of the United States in 1968. While in Oakland, California, he scheduled a meeting with African American community leaders. In a late-night meeting, he was called a hypocrite, out of touch, and a symbol of whiteness in the United States. Kennedy sat and listened. He did not get defensive or try to correct anyone. Kennedy reflected that Blacks had "a lot of hostility toward whites and lots of reasons for it. . . . They're just going to tell me off, over and over. I've been through these before, and you don't do anything. You listen and try to respond thoughtfully. But no matter how insulting they are, they're trying to communicate what's inside of them."[7] Later Kennedy said, "After all the abuse the Blacks have taken through the centuries, whites are just going to have to let them get some of these feelings out if we are ever going to settle down to a decent relationship."[8]

Robert Kennedy's willingness to listen without being defensive or centering the concerns of white people gained him supporters. The next day Kennedy returned to Oakland to campaign. Community leaders who participated in the meeting with Kennedy the night before were telling people to treat him with respect. Due to the massive crowds, the candidate's car could not move. The same people who had berated him at the meeting, including some Black Panthers, cleared a path so Kennedy's car could drive to his next stop. Whites must listen to truth spoken by BIPOC and stay in the conversation. Males must listen to truth from women in this #metoo season and stay in the conversation. Do not get defensive. Do not diminish another's truth. Do not personalize. Do not step away from the conversation table. That is a clear sign of privilege. People of Color and women cannot step away. Persist!

A Reconciliation Outcome

The Greek woman's approach to Jesus changed the conversation. Notice that Jesus said, "For such a reply you may go; the demon has left your daughter." Reconciliation was the outcome of this conversation between Jesus and the Greek woman from Syrian Phoenicia. "For such a reply . . ." Because she recognized her privilege and her own need, she also received healing. In the context of Roman oppression, Jews rarely trusted Greeks. The conversation between Jesus and the Greek woman was a first step in trust building. Trust became possible because she as a privileged, dominant-culture person acknowledged her privileged position, treated an oppressed Jew like Jesus with dignity and respect, and recognized her own need for healing.

For Jesus, this interaction produced hope that perhaps Greeks and Romans could experience transformation. It prompted Jesus to tour the Greek-populated areas of the region. From Tyre, he went to Sidon. Next, he spent three days in Decapolis, where he took loaves and fish and fed more than four thousand Greeks (Mark 7:31-36). Previously, he had fed five thousand Jews with twelve baskets left over—representing the twelve tribes of Israel (6:30-44). In Decapolis, seven baskets were left, which represented the seven Gentile nations. He used eucharistic language as he broke, blessed, and distributed the loaves of bread. Two feedings, using the language of the communion table, in separate ethnoreligious regions were a powerful symbol of reconciliation. In contexts of division and tension, conversations that welcome and embrace truth can produce reconciliation outcomes.

Notes

1. Robert H. Gundry, *Mark: A Commentary on His Apology for the Cross* (Grand Rapids, MI: Eerdmans, 1993), 376.

2. Richard A. Horsley, *Jesus and Empire: The Kingdom of God and the New World Disorder* (Minneapolis: Fortress, 2003), 15, 30.

3. A version of this episode is also found in Matthew 15:21-28. In Matthew's version the woman is identified as a Canaanite, rather than Greek or from Syrian Phoenicia. The identifiers "Greek" and "Canaanite" offer different options for interpretation. Most scholars consider Matthew's version as his "redactional product." See Robert A. Guelich, *Mark 1–8:26*, Word Biblical Commentary 34A (Dallas: Word Books, 1989), 383.

4. Wilda C. Gafney, *A Woman's Lectionary for the Whole Church: A Multi-Gospel Single-Year Lectionary* (New York: Church Publishing, 2021), 226.

5. From my research, I have not found "dog" used as a gender slur by first-century Jews. Obviously, this was a woman in a very patriarchal and misogynist society, and others have used gender as the primary lens for interpretation of this story. One of the most provocative and powerful examples comes from biblical scholar Wil Gafney, who used a womanist lens in her sermon on the Matthew text, "Drag Queens and Did Jesus Just Call That Woman a B—?", preached in 2012 (www.wilgafney.com/2012/09/12/drag-queens-and-did-jesus-just-call-that-woman-a-b/).

6. Miguel A. De La Torre, *The Politics of Jesús: A Hispanic Political Theology* (Lanham, MD: Rowman & Littlefield, 2015), 124–29. Like Gafney, De La Torre uses the Matthew text for his gender and race analysis. He offers a range of possibilities for Jesus' racism. For a discussion of the Matthew text as "antiracist womanist missiological literature" and a helpful comparison to the Mark text, see Love L. Sechrest, "'Humbled Among the Nations': Matthew 15:21-28 in Antiracist Womanist Missiological Engagement," in *Can "White" People Be Saved? Triangulating Race, Theology, and Mission*, ed. Love L. Sechrest, Johnny Ramírez-Johnson, and Amos Young (Downers Grove, IL: IVP Academic, 2018), 285–99.

7. Thurston Clarke, *The Last Campaign: Robert F. Kennedy and 82 Days that Inspired America* (New York: Henry Holt, 2008), 252.

8. Konstantin Sidorenko, *Robert F. Kennedy: A Spiritual Biography* (New York: Crossroad, 2000), 161.

CHAPTER 5

The Economics of Racial Equity

At present, however, I am going to Jerusalem in a ministry to the saints; for Macedonia and Achaia were pleased to share their resources with the poor among the saints at Jerusalem. They were pleased to do this, and indeed they owe it to them; for if the gentiles have come to share in their spiritual blessings, they ought also to be of service to them in material things. (Romans 15:25-27)

The twenty-first-century United States has much in common with the first-century setting described in the New Testament. Jews were a colonized and oppressed ethnic minority group under the rule of the Roman Empire. Due to Roman exceptionalism and a sense of supremacy, the prejudice Jews experienced led to economic deprivation. While this was true throughout the Roman Empire, it was especially evident in Palestine where the Jewish people were highly concentrated. Jews faced the oppressive realities of law enforcement. In addition, Jews in Jerusalem and greater Palestine experienced the military occupation of the empire. Thousands of Jews in Palestine were crucified by Roman state-sponsored killings. The emotions that are felt and expressed in the twenty-first century from the endless police killings of Black women and men in the United States—fear, rage, despondency—were certainly experienced by first-century Jews (and Jewish Christians).

These social realities likely caused extreme disparities among ethnic groups in the Roman Empire creating an economic reality that was comparable to our own racial context in the United States. The first-century church emerged in a reality of economic inequity based on ethnicity. The first followers of Jesus were primarily a Jewish community. Their churches met in the homes of Jewish Christians and were places of healing for Jews from the impact of colonialism and oppression (similar to the Black church in the United States).[1] The church spread into Jewish communities throughout the Roman Empire. At some point, Greeks and Romans were invited to join these Jewish churches. Romans and Greeks temporarily let go of their privileges, advantages, and entitlements to enter the homes of oppressed and colonized Jews for worship and community.

In Acts 10, we observe that Roman law enforcement officers joined these Jewish believers. A Roman centurion named Cornelius was invited by the apostle Peter to join the church. Theologian Willie Jennings notes, "If a centurion and his household could be drawn into a new circle of belonging, then its implications for challenging the claims of the Roman state were revolutionary."[2] Jennings's analysis offers a valuable perspective for consideration of the transformation of policing.

The New Testament model of the church was one where an oppressed minority community welcomed people from the privileged dominant culture into the local congregation.[3] These first-century faith communities were led by oppressed Jews. The Roman supremacist power dynamics structured into the empire had to be negotiated and negated inside the organizational systems of the first-century church once Greeks and Romans joined with Jewish followers of Jesus. An equity process that was introduced into the first-century church could be instructive for churches, denominations, and activist organizations in the United States in our times.

Equity in Times of Crisis

Many US Christian leaders looked to Scripture for insights and wisdom at the beginning of the COVID-19 health pandemic. This text addressing global famine offers a predicament with similar challenges:

> At that time prophets came down from Jerusalem to Antioch. One of them named Agabus stood up and predicted by the Spirit that there would be a severe famine over all the world, and this took place during the reign of Claudius. The disciples determined that, according to their ability, each would send relief to the brothers and sisters living in Judea; this they did, sending it to the elders by Barnabas and Saul. (Acts 11:27-30)

The Antioch congregation included privileged Greeks as members alongside oppressed Jews. Therefore, they had greater resources than the congregation in Jerusalem. The Antioch church raised money and sent it to their sisters and brothers in the faith in Jerusalem. The pre-existing economic challenges in that place were now exaggerated because there was a famine on the way.

As a former member of the Jerusalem church, Barnabas brought to Antioch a normative sense of equity from the mother church of Christianity in Jerusalem. They practiced a radical kind of sharing that generated equity among members within the congregation.

> Now the whole group of those who believed were of one heart and soul, and no one claimed private ownership of any possessions, but everything they owned was held in common. . . . There was not a needy person among them, for as many as owned lands or houses sold them and brought the proceeds of what was sold. They laid it at the

apostles' feet, and it was distributed to each as any had need. There was a Levite, a native of Cyprus, Joseph, to whom the apostles gave the name Barnabas (which means "son of encouragement"). He sold a field that belonged to him, then brought the money, and laid it at the apostles' feet. (Acts 4:32, 34-37)

The practice of building equitable relationships within the congregation was integrated into the definition of what it meant to follow Jesus and participate in the life of the Jerusalem church. Barnabas, residing in Antioch, expanded the notion of equity when a famine occurred in Jerusalem. The internal congregational practice of Jerusalem expanded to a congregation-to-congregation transfer of resources. A congregation of means in Antioch sent funds to a congregation in need in Jerusalem facing a crisis. Similarly, many examples of crisis funding during the COVID-19 pandemic occurred, ranging from technological support for congregations with less tech savvy to financial resources for congregations where the COVID-19 pandemic devastated their already meager budgets.

Immediately following the killing of George Floyd in Minneapolis, Black neighborhoods that were already food deserts had their grocery stores and pharmacies damaged and destroyed by white supremacist vigilantes. White congregations provided food, transportation, and money to Black churches. Charitable actions can address inequities that are multiplied in times of crisis and serve as a demonstration that all churches belong to the same spiritual family.

Equity also involves how the process is managed. Barnabas and Saul personally delivered the offering to the elders in Jerusalem (the apostles Peter, James, and John) in an action that expressed respect for equity in leadership. The leaders of the better-resourced church sent their lead pastors to personally deliver the money to the lead pastors at the congregation in need. An associate mission pastor was not sent to meet with the senior pastor of the affected church. Such an action might imply that the Jerusalem church was a mission project of the Antioch church rather than an equal partner. Equity in leadership interaction is essential to an authentic equity process. Equity relationships between local congregations are rare today. Yet in moments of crisis, charitable instincts create opportunities to address the increased equity gaps that form on top of the already pre-existing disparities.

Systemic Equity as a Core Value

Deeply rooted systemic disparities are not remedied by crisis responses. The reality that Jerusalem church members faced daily economic challenges rooted in systemic inequities in society was not transformed by the Antioch church's monetary provision. The generosity of the Antioch church, in a season of global famine, was a one-time act of charity.

Some are calling for a program of reparations to address the persistent equity gaps in US society. The church can be a moral voice in society when it steps into its prophetic role. Should the church use its moral authority to call for reparations for Black and Indigenous people in the United States?[4] Economists William A. Darity Jr. and A. Kirsten Mullen use the acronym ARC, which stands for acknowledgment, redress, and closure, to advocate for a process of addressing historic racial disparities.[5] According to them, reparations are effective when "an improved position for Blacks [and Native Americans] is associated with sharp and enduring reductions in racial disparities, particularly economic disparities like racial wealth inequality, and corresponding sharp and enduring improvements in Black [and Native American] well-being."[6]

Before calling for national reparations, the church must acknowledge that the same racial disparities that are evident in society exist in the church. Predominately white denominations generally are significantly better resourced than historic Black denominations in the United States. White congregations are typically better off than their BIPOC counterparts of similar size. The church does not have the credibility to call for reparations in society unless it addresses its own racial inequities.

In the first-century church, the economic gaps in society between privileged Greeks and Romans and oppressed Jews were also fully evident. Paul and Barnabas met again with the leaders in Jerusalem—Peter, James the brother of Jesus, and John—sometime after they delivered the Antioch monetary relief package to the Jerusalem church (Galatians 2:9-10). The meeting was to discern how to not lose the Jewish presence and voice with the growing numbers of Greeks and Romans joining the church. Paul and Barnabas were asked by the apostle James to "remember the poor" (2:10). The growing and more prosperous congregations that included (at times were dominated by) Greeks and Romans needed to establish some sort of equity or reparations relationship with the economically challenged predominately Jewish populated congregations in Palestine. Paul and Barnabas were "eager to do" this (2:10).

We read in the apostle Paul's letters that he did indeed respond to the request of the leaders from the Jerusalem church, not leaving "community values of mutuality and solidarity in the abstract."[7] He organized a collection of money for the Jerusalem church from churches in Galatia, Macedonia, Achaia, and Asia that he started in the Greek-speaking world of the Roman Empire.[8] He described this initiative in his letter to the Romans: "At present, however, I am going to Jerusalem in a ministry to the saints; for Macedonia and Achaia were pleased to share their resources with the poor among the saints at Jerusalem. They were pleased to do this, and indeed they owe it to them; for if the gentiles have come to share in their spiritual blessings, they ought also to be of service to them in material things" (Romans 15:25-27).

For Paul, this was a central priority of his ministry. He delayed a planned visit to Spain until after he delivered the collection to Jerusalem (Romans 15:23-25). This was not a one-time, crisis-based response. I believe he was creating a system-wide action for "the divine equity of distributive justice" in his churches.[9] Paul even suggested that funds for Jerusalem be set aside weekly (1 Corinthians 16:1-2). We do not know the outcome of this project. Expanding on the Jerusalem church's practice of an internal sharing to build community equity, Paul was creating a global church-wide practice of equity—an ongoing equity mechanism for the church to express its unity.

Even more remarkable is that Paul saw this as a reciprocal act.[10] He believed that Roman and Greek Christians were in debt because they received "spiritual blessings" from Jewish Christians who introduced them to Jesus Christ. Therefore, they needed to reciprocate with what Jewish Christians in Jerusalem needed, "material things." Greeks and Romans should support materially Jewish Christians (economic reparations) because they received the gospel from the Jewish church. Paul believed this should be "understood as an act of mutual concern between Christian equals."[11] While the work of racial equity was a justice initiative, for Paul economic reparations were also implemented based on relational reciprocity. The Greek and Roman Christians owed this to Jewish Christians. As the *First Nations Version* reads in Romans 15:27, "For since the Outside Nations have shared in the spiritual blessings of the Tribal People, they are bound by honor to also share their material blessings with them—which they do with glad hearts!"[12]

When Greek and Roman Christians joined the church founded by Jewish Christians and embraced a Jewish Christ, they received spiritual blessings. These spiritual blessings were experienced as they gained freedom from the dehumanizing effects of colonialism and a Roman supremacy identity. Identity in Jesus Christ replaced their Roman colonial identity. Through the death on a cross and resurrection of Jesus, Romans and Greeks with power and privilege were transformed by God's reconciling grace. First-century Jewish followers of Jesus looked through the distortions of domination and colonization and saw the humanity of Romans and Greeks. An identity rooted in Christ and the liberation from a colonial supremacist mindset were spiritual blessings for Greeks and Romans. Paul was inviting Romans and Greeks to reciprocate so that Jewish Christians would receive the needed material blessing of economic support. Equity was reciprocal.

A Reciprocal Equity Today

Denominations and congregations in the United States mirror the racial disparities in broader society. The integrity of the US church as a moral voice for reparations, justice, and equity is compromised by its own internal issues of inequity. The apostle Paul's creation of an ongoing equity mechanism in the church is relevant today. White denominations and congregations of means must choose to invest in creating economic equity with BIPOC churches.

In *White Too Long: The Legacy of White Supremacy in American Christianity*, sociologist Robert P. Jones writes:

> Christian theology and institutions have been the central cultural tent pole holding up the very idea of white supremacy. And the genetic imprint of this legacy remains present and measurable in contemporary white Christianity . . . After centuries of complicity, the norms of white supremacy have become deeply and broadly integrated into white Christian identity, operating far below the level of consciousness. To many well-meaning white

> Christians today—evangelical Protestant, mainline Protestant, and Catholic—Christianity and a cultural norm of white supremacy now often feel indistinguishable.[13]

According to Jones, present-day white Christianity carries the "genetic imprint" of white supremacy. The first-century Jewish church liberated Greeks and Romans from the genetic imprint of Roman supremacist captivity. Twenty-first-century US white Christianity has been formed by white supremacy, and it empowers a racist system to continue to flourish. BIPOC Christians are relegated to an economically inferior position in society (and the church) and a second-class Christianity in the minds of too many whites.

The church began in Jerusalem as a community of colonized, oppressed, ethnic minority Jews. They experienced spiritual healing through Jesus Christ and invited those who had benefited from their oppression to also experience healing that was the essence of biblical reconciliation (Ephesians 2).[14] Greek and Roman Christians were invited to invest financially in the Jewish church in exchange for this spiritual blessing.

The question must be posed: Can white Christianity free itself from the captivity of white supremacy? Does white Christianity need the investment of a spiritual blessing from the faith found in Black, Indigenous, Latine, and Asian churches to be healed of whiteness? Are white churches dependent on BIPOC Christians for the hope of their salvation? (Do similar questions need to be asked of predominately white activist organizations?)

White Christians must invest in repairing the race-based economic inequities in the church. Many churches in Black, Indigenous, Asian, and Latine communities need additional resources for their ministries to thrive. Present-day white Christianity needs a spiritual investment from BIPOC churches to be healed from the genetic imprint of racism. The church needs relationally reciprocal equity like that initiated in the first century by the apostle Paul. This is the economics of racial equity.

Notes

1. For more on my view of the first-century church as a decolonizing and healing community, see Allan Aubrey Boesak and Curtiss Paul DeYoung, *Radical Reconciliation: Beyond Political Pietism and Christian Quietism* (Maryknoll, NY: Orbis Books, 2012), 12–23, 79–83; Curtiss Paul DeYoung, Jacqueline J. Lewis, Micky ScottBey Jones, Robyn Afrik, Sarah Thompson Nahar, Sindy Morales Garcia, and 'Iwalani Ka'ai, *Becoming Like Creoles: Living and Leading at the Intersections of Injustice, Culture, and Religion* (Minneapolis: Fortress, 2019), 1–15.

2. Willie James Jennings, *The Christian Imagination: Theology and the Origins of Race* (New Haven, CT: Yale University Press, 2010), 269.

3. Boesak and DeYoung, 79–83.

4. See David Crary, "More US Churches Are Committing to Racism-Linked Reparations," Associated Press, December 13, 2020, www.apnews.com/article/race-and-ethnicity-new-york-slavery-minnesota-native-americans-4c7dbcae990bd11dee5a5710c63ece25.

5. William A. Darity Jr. and A. Kirsten Mullen, *From Here to Equality: Reparations for Black Americans in the Twenty-First Century* (Chapel Hill: University of North Carolina Press, 2020), 2–3.

6. Ibid., 3.

7. Neil Elliot, *Liberating Paul: The Justice of God and the Politics of the Apostle* (Minneapolis: Fortress, 2006), 201.

8. See also 1 Corinthians 16:1-4; 2 Corinthians 8:1–9:15; Galatians 2:10. For an overview of Paul's collection for Jerusalem, see Paul B. Duff, "Focus On: Paul's Collection for the Poor in Jerusalem," *Oxford Biblical Studies Online*, https://global.oup.com/obso/focus/focus_on_paul_collection/.

9. John Dominic Crossan and Jonathan L. Reed, *In Search of Paul: How Jesus's Apostle Opposed Rome's Empire with God's Kingdom* (San Francisco: HarperSanFranciso, 2004), 355.

10. N. T. Wright, "The Letter to the Romans," in *The New Interpreter's Bible* 10, ed. Leander E. Keck (Nashville: Abingdon, 2002), 756.

11. James D. G. Dunn, *Romans 9–16*, Word Biblical Commentary 38B (Grand Rapids, MI: Zondervan, 1988), 874.

12. *First Nations Version: An Indigenous Translation of the New Testament* (Downers Grove, IL: InterVarsity Press, 2021), 296.

13. Robert P. Jones, *White Too Long: The Legacy of White Supremacy in American Christianity* (New York: Simon & Schuster, 2020), 6, 10.

14. Boesak and DeYoung, 11–16.

CHAPTER 6

The Complexities of Ending Empire

> For if you keep silent at this time, relief and deliverance will rise for the Jews from another place, but you and your father's family will perish. Who knows? Perhaps you have come to royal dignity for just such a time as this. (Esther 4:14)

The narrative journey of Queen Esther is rightfully considered a story of courage to be aspired to for "such a time as this." The Book of Esther is a story of empire and colonization; oppressed folks trying to survive; racial hatred and threats of ethnic genocide; women who resist gender, economic, and racial injustice; and a people a long way from their homeland living a diasporic existence. But a closer look at the entire book reveals a complicated narrative and a mix of characters who are sometimes heroic and other times compromising. The biblical story exposes the complexities of our attempts to bring justice to the empire.

The story of Esther takes place in the Persian Empire—which at the time ruled nearly the entire world known to biblical writers from Ethiopia to India. Persia was the world's sole superpower. The leader of the Persian Empire was a narcissist of sorts named King Xerxes. In the Hebrew text of the Book of Esther, he is called King Ahasuerus, which is the Hebrew word for "mighty man." This is a title that King Xerxes gave himself. The king had his self-given name "mighty man" inscribed on edifices all across the empire.[1]

King Xerxes controlled the world. So, what do kings do when they have conquered all there is to conquer? Well, King Xerxes hosted a party. It was a six-month-long party, where he displayed all the wealth and glamour of the empire. On the final day of the party, he wanted to display the crowning glory of his wealth and splendor. He ordered his queen, Vashti, to put on her crown, come to the gathering, and parade in front of all the male officials and guests so they could admire the beauty of Xerxes's queen. Queen Vashti refused King Xerxes's orders. No one ever refused the king. Her denial of Xerxes's request resulted in the loss of her crown. And Vashti disappeared from the story.

King Xerxes needed a new queen. The king's staff organized a beauty pageant, a Miss Universe contest. Four hundred teenage virgin girls were recruited to compete.[2] They were put through a year-long beautification process as a member of the king's harem. Of the four hundred, only one would be chosen queen. The selection process was simple. Each young girl would spend a night with King Xerxes. He would choose one of the four hundred to be his queen. The other three hundred ninety-nine would be sent to the harem of the concubines and live out the remainder of their lives as though they were widows—never to marry. It was a high-stakes contest. A young Jewish girl named Hadassah entered the beauty contest using the Persian name Esther. Her cousin and adoptive father, Mordecai, encouraged her to enter and use a Persian name. She was the one selected from among the four hundred. She became Queen Esther, the wife of King Xerxes.

Let's pause for a moment of analysis and reflection. This story is very problematic! First, using a gender lens, this was a story where the women, Vashti and Esther, were used to "achieve [a] male agenda."[3] Whatever wealth, power, and influence they had was derived from their marriage to King Xerxes. They used their beauty and their bodies to become the chosen queen. Second, using a race and ethnicity lens, this was a story about assimilation and loss of identity. Esther's cousin and adoptive father, Mordecai, instructed Esther not to reveal that she was a Jew. She needed to pass as a Persian in order to be the queen. Esther became the first Jewish queen of Persia under the cloak of secrecy. Esther's identity was securely hidden. No one could know she was Jewish. Over time, as noted preacher Jeremiah A. Wright Jr. proclaimed, "Esther forgot who she was."[4] Third, using a lens of ethics and morality, this was a story of a father (Mordecai) who sent his daughter (Esther) into a beauty contest where the young, sheltered, virgin girl must join a harem and earn the position of queen by having sex with a much older male king. This story is troubling. Without any expression of ethical concern or moral trepidation, the author of the Book of Esther narrated "the sexual exploitation of young girls."[5]

One more important incident precedes our text that is essential to understand this story. Esther's adoptive father, Mordecai, was an official in King Xerxes's Persian government. While Esther had become queen, Mordecai was causing some controversy. King Xerxes's second-in-command was named Haman. It was official protocol, ordered by the king, to bow down to Haman when he passed by. Mordecai refused to bow to Haman. His reasons were not noted in the text, yet Mordecai's actions were experienced as a personal slight by Haman. He learned that Mordecai was a Jew and decided to apply collective punishment by killing all the Jews.[6] He convinced King Xerxes to pass racist antisemitic legislation that would order the extermination of all Jews. Xerxes approved of Haman's plans without a second thought. The casual racism and brutality of the king are shocking.

Mordecai learned of Haman's intentions and warned his adoptive daughter Queen Esther, "Do not think that in the king's palace you will escape any more than all the other Jews" (4:13). Then Mordecai appealed to Esther: "For if you keep silent at this time, relief and deliverance will rise for the Jews from another place, but you and your father's family will perish. Who knows? Perhaps you have come to royal dignity for just such a time as this" (4:14).

Prior Resistance

The story of Esther would not exist if the drama did not begin with an act of resistance. King Xerxes had ordered Queen Vashti to put on her crown and come to the party. Some rabbinical commentators believe that Xerxes ordered Vashti to appear naked wearing only her crown.[7] She refused to be objectified before a room full of men. Vashti resisted and rebelled against the all-powerful King Xerxes. We often miss this moment and skip ahead to Esther. Preaching professor Melva L. Sampson notes that this was a "monumental moment of liberation . . . the making of a model of leadership." My Howard University School of Divinity classmate Bishop Vashti Murphy McKenzie became the first woman bishop in the African Methodist Episcopal Church because she had a similar resolve and ethical character as her biblical namesake. Sampson further reminds us that we also "will have to choose between revolution and apathy, between objectification and humiliation, and between the inevitability of pain and the option of misery."[8]

The text tells us that Mordecai actively resisted the anti-Jewish legislation sponsored by Haman. Although he had told Esther to pass as Persian, and he was known by a Babylonian name, he reclaimed his Jewish ethnic identity and protested in the streets on behalf of all Jews. The Jews all around the country joined him. "Mordecai tore his clothes and put on sackcloth and ashes and went through the city, wailing with a loud and bitter cry; he went up to the entrance of the king's gate, for no one might enter the king's gate clothed with sackcloth. In every province . . . there was great mourning among the Jews . . . and most of them lay in sackcloth and ashes" (4:1-3).

The prior resistance of Vashti and Mordecai set the foundation for Esther's act of resistance. And for such a time as this, at great risk, Esther appealed to the king against Haman. She shed her assimilated Persian persona and embraced her real identity as a Jew. She risked losing her privilege and power to appeal to the king on behalf of all Jews. As Esther said to Mordecai in a message, "If any man or woman goes to the king inside the inner court without being called, there is but one law: to be put to death. Only if the king holds out the golden scepter to someone may that person live" (4:11). Esther risked her own death: "If I perish, I perish" (4:16). But if she did not approach the king, she might also die as a Jew with the rest of her community.

Such a time as this requires that we show up, stand up, and speak out. Dr. Martin Luther King Jr. said, "A time comes when silence is betrayal."[9] Vashti was completely powerless as a woman, yet she exercised the power of refusal. Mordecai challenged the hate directed at Jews through the power of protest. Esther used her position of privilege to approach the king through the power of access. What power do we have that can be used to challenge the injustice in our time?

Present Danger

As biblical scholar Sidnie Crawford writes, "The book of Esther explores . . . racial hatred, the threat of genocide, and the evil of overweening pride and vanity."[10] Xerxes was a narcissist, racist, nationalist king. Haman had launched an ethnic cleansing edict to kill all Jews in the name of King Xerxes. The edict became law. Mordecai sounded the alarm through protest against the planned genocide of the Jews that had been set in motion in Persia. The resistance of Vashti, Mordecai, and Esther was in the context of a very present danger.

The danger of empire-like realities of white supremacy and white nationalism plague the United States. This causes the present dangers of the killing of Blacks by racialized police forces, disappearances of Native women, rounding up of immigrants, attempts to limit refugee arrivals, and building border walls. The growing reality of white male vigilantes attacking, shooting, and killing Blacks, Native Americans, Asians, Latine, Muslims, Jews, and women in grocery stores, places of worship, while jogging, and just living life is alarming. There is a present danger in our nation and in our various locales! Let us name the dangers. Let us tell the stories of our forerunners in resistance—the Vashtis, Mordecais, and Esthers in our time and place. And let us be the present-day resistance force as we face an ever-present danger.

Preparatory Placement

Esther becoming queen prepared her to be in the right place at the right time for a needed future action. She did not know when she became queen what would be required of her. "Perhaps you have come to royal dignity for just such a time as this." In her cloistered life as queen, she may have been unaware of Haman's edict. Yet, once she learned from Mordecai what was at stake, she acted with great courage. The story continued with an elaborate plan by Esther that exposed Haman's murderous intentions. Haman was put to death by the king on gallows that were built by Haman to execute Mordecai. But the genocidal, racist, antisemitic legislation was still in place. Esther appealed to the king to have it changed. King Xerxes told Esther and Mordecai to rewrite the rules. The success of the story hinged on Esther's preparatory placement as queen.

Empires write oppression into the rules of conduct and governance. In the United States, racism is woven throughout the structures of life—we call it systemic racism. To transform a society, the racist rules must be overhauled. The civil rights protests of the 1950s and early 1960s ended segregation in public places in the United States. But the Civil Rights Act of 1964 rewrote the laws regarding segregation. The Civil Rights Act of 1964 outlawed discrimination based on race, color, religion, sex, and national origin. Some of us must prepare for this work by placing ourselves in the work of community organizing for public policy change that must accompany our sermonic soundings, outcry, and protest.

Problematic Temptation

As I read further in the story, I noticed how carefully Esther and Mordecai rewrote the legislation. Xerxes had told them, "You may write as you please with regard to the Jews, in the name of the king" (8:8). Esther and Mordecai removed all the clauses that called for the destruction of the Jews. Then, they added this clause: Jews were allowed to "kill, and to annihilate any armed force of any people or province that might attack them, with their children and women, and to plunder their goods" (8:11). Esther and Mordecai enabled Jews to defend themselves. But they also allowed for revenge that included killing women and children (8:13). Over the course of two days, more than seventy-five thousand people in the Persian Empire were killed. And the massacre was celebrated. The Book of Esther ends with Esther and Mordecai securely entrenched in the leadership of the Persian Empire. They took Haman's plan to kill all Jews and turned it on his family and followers. They took Haman's power in the empire and made it their own, joining the ruling elite. Mordecai took Haman's position as the second-in-command in the empire (10:3). Esther and Mordecai became that which they had resisted against by supporting "the maintenance of the oppressive system, since they dare not challenge that system itself."[11]

Too often, we become that which we are struggling to transform. Activists who become elected officials must be held accountable by their communities to remain justice focused. Moving up into more powerful positions of leadership in social justice organizations does not guarantee we will act for justice. Persons who have been oppressed in society can be co-opted by new power and influence. Decisions made by women in leadership can privilege men. Decisions made by BIPOC in leadership can privilege whites. Social justice-minded white or male activists can compromise their anti-racist or feminist agenda when they become the CEO of the organization. By taking positions of leadership so we can make a bigger difference, we can create a chasm between us in our now more privileged position and those directly facing the brunt of oppression. The comforts and privileges of positional status often lead to comfort with privilege and an embrace of subtle ways of maintaining power. We may sit with and even become friends with those who benefit from the empire. The story of Esther and Mordecai should be a warning of the problematic temptations that accompany advancement in leadership, success in fundraising, media attention, and the like.[12]

Primary Allegiance

Nowhere in the Book of Esther is God mentioned. God was not a part of this story. There was no record of action by God. There was no mention of prayer, the temple, Jerusalem, the exodus, Israel, or anything that would show evidence of a role for God or an awareness of God in the story. "The secularity of the book" has troubled translators, rabbis, and Christian scholars.[13] Later translators inserted references to God and prayer into the text.[14] Early Christians debated its canonical status. The Book of Esther was never quoted in the New Testament. It was not included in any Christian commentaries before the year 700, and neither Martin

Luther nor John Calvin offered commentary on the Book of Esther.[15] Luther disliked the book.[16]

It is what was not in the story that provides us with a final point of what is required to end empire. We must not leave God out of the story. Before nation, people, culture, and family, God must be our primary allegiance. The Book of Esther ends with the empire still operating much as it always had. Esther and Mordecai were seated in influential positions of managing the affairs and structures of an unjust system ruled by a narcissistic king. Their acts of resistance were not sustained at the level of their values because missing from the transformation equation was the active presence of God. May we be inspired by the acts of resistance by Vashti, Mordecai, and Esther with the added insistence that God is central in the effort to end empire.

Notes

1. Sidnie White Crawford, "The Book of Esther," in *The New Interpreter's Bible* vol. 3, ed. Leander E. Keck (Nashville: Abingdon, 1999), 878.

2. The number four hundred comes from Josephus, *Antiquities of the Jews*, XI, 201, cited in Crawford, 888.

3. Dorothy Bea Akoto (née Abutiate), "Esther," in *The Africana Bible: Reading Israel's Scriptures from Africa and the African Diaspora*, Hugh R. Page, general ed. (Minneapolis: Fortress, 2010), 268.

4. Jeremiah A. Wright Jr., *What Makes You So Strong?: Sermons of Joy and Strength*, ed. Jini Kilgore Ross (Valley Forge, PA: Judson Press, 1993), 66.

5. Cheryl B. Anderson, *Ancient Laws and Contemporary Controversies: The Need for Inclusive Biblical Interpretation* (New York: Oxford University Press, 2009), 67.

6. There was a history of animosity between Haman's people, the Agagites, and the Jews.

7. Crawford, 882.

8. Melva L. Sampson, "Hell No!", in Kimberly P. Johnson, *The Womanist Preacher: Proclaiming Womanist Rhetoric from the Pulpit* (London: Lexington Books, 2017), 146.

9. Martin Luther King Jr., "A Time to Break Silence," in *A Testament of Hope: The Essential Writings and Speeches of Martin Luther King Jr.*, ed. James M. Washington (San Francisco: HarperSanFrancisco, 1986), 231.

10. Crawford, 855.

11. Anderson, 70.

12. For more on the need for accountability, see Allan Aubrey Boesak and Curtiss Paul DeYoung, *Radical Reconciliation: Beyond Political Pietism and Christian Quietism* (Maryknoll, NY: Orbis Books, 2012), 115–29.

13. Frederic Bush, *Ruth–Esther*, Word Biblical Commentary 9 (Grand Rapids, MI: Zondervan, 1996), 275.

14. Crawford, 955–60; includes the actual additions made.

15. Joyce G. Baldwin, *Esther: An Introduction and Commentary* (Downers Grove, IL: InterVarsity Press, 1984), 32.

16. Crawford, 868.

CHAPTER 7

Called Out of Egypt

When Israel was a child, I loved him, and out of Egypt I called my son. (Hosea 11:1)

Now after they had left, an angel of the Lord appeared to Joseph in a dream and said, "Get up, take the child and his mother, and flee to Egypt, and remain there until I tell you; for Herod is about to search for the child, to destroy him." Then Joseph got up, took the child and his mother by night, and went to Egypt and remained there until the death of Herod. This was to fulfill what had been spoken by the Lord through the prophet, "Out of Egypt I have called my son." (Matthew 2:13-15)

Liberation

In the early part of the history of the Hebrew people, God was referred to as the God of Abraham, Isaac, and Jacob. Today, we also add the God of Hagar, Sarah, Rebekah, Leah, and Rachel. The people related to God through their leaders—the patriarchs and matriarchs of faith. This all changed when the ancient Israelites were liberated by God from the oppressive slavery they endured under Pharaoh while held captive in Egypt. No longer was this just a religion of the leaders. Everyone had experienced God's liberation. We hear this so clearly in the way God was identified in the first of the Ten Commandments. "I am the LORD your God, who brought you out of the land of Egypt, out of the house of slavery;

you shall have no other gods before me" (Exodus 20:2-3). When Hosea originally uttered the words "out of Egypt I called my son," it was an expression of the Hebrew people's central understanding of God. Hosea referred to Israel as God's son. Israel had been liberated from Egypt. Hosea's God was a God of liberation.

The Hosea text jumped through time into the reading of the first-century church. The leaders of the first-century church and the Gospel writers were reading their Scriptures through the lens of the Jesus story. Suddenly, texts that had always said one thing now said something new because they were reading the Hebrew Scriptures through their experience of Jesus. As they read Hosea's words on God's son being called out of Egypt, they interpreted it as referring to God's Son Jesus and his emergence out of Egypt as a child.

Hosea wrote of God liberating ancient Israel from Pharaoh's Egypt. The Gospel writer Matthew spoke of God liberating Jesus from the threats and killing rage of King Herod by sending Jesus and his parents into Egypt. For Hosea, Egypt was a place of slavery and oppression. For Matthew, Egypt was a place of escape, safety, and refuge from King Herod's murderous intentions, "a classic land of refuge for those fleeing tyranny in Palestine."[1] Biblical scholar R. T. France notes, "Egypt, the southwestern neighbor of Judea and now a Roman province with a large Jewish population especially in Alexandria, was a natural place for Jews to seek asylum when in political danger at home."[2] The historical Herod the Great was ruthless and followed up on his threats. He killed numerous political rivals including three of his sons, a brother-in-law, a mother-in-law, and a wife.[3]

Both Hosea and Matthew were announcing that God is a God of liberation, whether from Pharaoh or King Herod. Egypt represented a narrative of liberation whether it was a place of bondage under Pharaoh or a place of refuge from Herod. Matthew was connecting the ministry of Jesus to the Hosea tradition of liberation. For the first-century church, the message and leadership of Jesus were centrally focused on liberation. At his inaugural sermon in Nazareth Jesus announced, "The Spirit of the Lord is upon me, because he has anointed me to bring good news to the poor. He has sent me to proclaim release to the captives and recovery of sight to the blind, to set free those who are oppressed, to proclaim the year of the Lord's favor" (Luke 4:18-19; see also Isaiah 61:1-2).

Hold onto the word *liberation*.

Affirmation

The text jumped from Hosea into the Gospel of Matthew, and the first-century context changed how the ancient text was interpreted. The text jumped again. This time it jumped from the Gospel of Matthew into the context of the slave quarters of Africans kidnapped and brought to North America and into the context of African American churches, which had emerged because of the racism of white Christians. This new context was one of race-based slavery, Jim Crow segregation, and systemic racism—all the result of white supremacy.

Slavery and racial segregation were considered God-ordained realities by many white Christians. All the pictures in the Bible were of white people.[4] It was as though Black people and Africans were left out of God's salvation story. But when Blacks, oppressed by slavery and segregation, heard the text "out of Egypt I have called my son," they heard, "Out of AFRICA I have called my son Jesus." Their context changed the interpretation of the text. During his years as the pastor of Bethel African Methodist Episcopal Church in Baltimore, Bishop Frank Madison Reid III preached from this Matthew text and declared that "Jesus had an African connection."[5]

It was not unusual in the Hebrew Scriptures for "Egypt" to be a reference for broader Africa and not just the nation of Egypt. In Psalm 105, Egypt is interchangeable with "the land of Ham" (a reference to Africa). Even the new *First Nations Version* translates

Matthew 2 as "I will call my son out from Black Land (Egypt)."[6] The fact that Jesus had lived in Africa was a message of affirmation to people of African descent who were told they were inferior to whites, using a white Jesus as the evidence.

Soon African American biblical scholars began to look more closely at the Bible. Genesis begins with a garden located in Africa, in present-day Sudan. Two of the four rivers that surrounded the Garden of Eden were in Africa (Genesis 2:10-13). Those rivers were the Pishon and Gihon, today known as the Blue and White Nile rivers.[7] Black scholars dismissed and disproved the claims that Black people were cursed as descendants of Ham or Cain. Neither was cursed.[8] Black scholars researched the Scriptures and determined that people and places from the continent of Africa were mentioned more than 850 times in the Bible.[9] Afrocentric scholars examined the genealogy of the Hebrew people and Jesus. They discovered Africans among the ancestors. Jesus and the Hebrew people were Afro-Asiatic.[10] The narrative in Matthew accompanying our text has Jesus, Mary, and Joseph traveling to Egypt to hide from King Herod. If they were Northern European whites as portrayed in the Bible pictures (and paintings), they could never hide in Africa. The presence of Africa and Black people in the Bible was a statement of God's affirmation for a people who had for generations experienced the pervasive degradation of racist lies.

I learned all of this from my Bible professors at Howard University School of Divinity (a historically Black divinity school).[11] I was invited to speak at a multiracial Christian gathering in South Africa. I decided I would share what I had learned from Black biblical scholars. In attendance were people from all four racial groups as defined under South African apartheid: Black indigenous Africans (from many ethnic and cultural groups), Coloureds (Khoisan and people of mixed-race descent), Indians (originally from India), and whites (Afrikaans and English speaking). I was shocked to discover that in South Africa, on the continent of

Africa, the extensive presence of Africans in the Bible seemed unknown. A church leader proclaimed, "I am finally able to say that I am proud to be both Black and a Christian!" A youth worker from the township of Soweto stated, "Discovering that there are Africans in the Bible is empowering. Christianity is not the white man's religion!"[12]

When I shared the racial and cultural heritage of the historic Jesus of Nazareth as Afro-Asiatic, this again was a new revelation. All the participants accepted that Jesus was a white European because of the white images they had observed since childhood. This moment was so joyous and affirming that Black indigenous Africans in my seminar stood up and in an impromptu celebration danced the militant and liberative toyi-toyi as they embraced the Black African Jesus. The point I am making is that when the Matthew text jumped from the Gospel narrative of the first century into African American communities in the United States and churches in Africa and the broader African diaspora as well, the text offered a powerful word of affirmation and truth. I have repeatedly observed this affirmative effect when the truth of the African/Black presence in the Scriptures was shared by Black biblical scholars like my mentor Cain Hope Felder—and even when a white hermeneutician like myself has shared this truth on the continent of Africa, in African diaspora churches in Guadeloupe, or in African American congregations in the United States.

Hold onto the word *affirmation*.

Transformation

The text jumped from Hosea into the Gospel of Matthew and the context of the first-century church. Then the text jumped again from the Gospel of Matthew into the hearts and minds of Black preachers interpreting the Scripture text in a context of slavery, segregation, and racism. We are now in the third decade of the twenty-first century. When the text jumps into our context, what does it say to us? What is the Egypt that we are being called out of?

I have introduced three Egypts: Hosea's Egypt, Matthew's Egypt, and the Black church's Africa. Hosea's Egypt referred to the call out of Pharaoh's captivity and to the liberation journey to the Promised Land. Some of us need to hear Hosea's God calling us out of oppression into liberation. The future promise of liberation is waiting. Matthew's Egypt was also a call, after Herod's death, out of a place of refuge, safety, and healing. After a time of rest and recovery, circumstances changed, and it was time to return. But not a return to Bethlehem, where another Herod awaited. Go to a new place—go to Nazareth. Some of us need to hear Matthew's God calling us to embrace our liberation and recovery and return to the struggle. The Black church's Egypt/Africa was a call to reclaim Black identity as created in the image of God. It was a call out of the lies of anti-Blackness into the truth of "Black Lives Matter" affirmation. Some of us need to hear the Black church's God calling us to affirm Blackness.

I am composing the final section of this reflection on the second anniversary of the death of George Floyd. I suggest that, in our time, the text jumps into the context of George Floyd Square. The global images of people from all races and cultures protesting awakened us to the possibilities of racial reckoning and the promise of multiracial transformation. France notes, "Including Egypt in the story of Jesus's infancy is to add an important extra dimension to the geographical area which is involved in preparing for the coming Messiah. Not only is he the Galilean Messiah born in Judea, but he is honored by Magi from 'the East' . . . and part of his childhood is spent in safety in Egypt."[13] Jesus was born a Jew in Palestine, visited by Asian Magi, and lived in Africa until God called him out of Egypt. No ethnic group, no nation, no race of people can own Jesus. The Jesus story is bigger than any one nation, cultural group, or people. Yet, George Floyd Square speaks of a multiracial call rooted in Black lived experience.

A few years ago, the Academy Awards ceremony announced that the best picture was for the movie *Green Book*. Following the ceremony, Michael Barbaro of the *New York Times* news show "The Daily" interviewed Black film critic Wesley Morris for his perspective on the controversy surrounding the choice of *Green Book* as the best picture. Morris started by saying that the quality of the filmmaking was not in question. The concerns that had risen had to do with how the story of the Green Book phenomenon during Jim Crow racial segregation was told. Morris said that movie had created a "racial reconciliation fantasy." The story was told from a white perspective, on the terms of white people. Nothing in the film addressed the social systems that maintain racism and keep us divided. The story was a portrayal of how Black people can be inserted into the pervasive and defining narrative of whiteness in US society—in other words, a racial reconciliation fantasy.[14]

The narrative of the killing of George Floyd and the multiracial response must be told from the lens of Black lived experience. Otherwise, it can become a racial reconciliation fantasy. A few days after the death of Floyd, well-intentioned artists painted the iconic mural of George Floyd on the side of Cup Foods, just a few feet from where he was killed. None of the artists were Black. Quickly, Black community artists and activists in Minneapolis criticized the mural artists for "taking such a prominent position in a space that community members dedicated to the expression of Black perspectives . . . it didn't represent the people most affected by Floyd's killing." A conversation emerged about representation and "who's creating the art at the heart of the movement, and why that matters."[15] Black artists stepped in to make it right and populated the rest of the square with art that came from Black lived experience. Even Floyd's facial features in the original version of the mural were made more accurate by Black artists.[16]

The killing of George Floyd ignited an international response to oppression and racialized policing, and it sounded a global call for racial justice and equity. In the United States, protests occurred in all fifty states in cities and towns for weeks following. Solidarity protests were observed in Canada, Europe, Africa, and Asia. These focused on racism and policing in the US but also brought renewed attention to racism that existed in the countries where the protests took place.

Eight days after the death of George Floyd, a silent clergy march to George Floyd Square was led by Black clergy from Minneapolis and St. Paul. Following Black clergy were religious leaders from all faith traditions with leaders of color behind the Black clergy and whites behind the BIPOC faith leaders. This march was intentionally designed to portray a vision of Black clergy leadership with whites having the backs of BIPOC religious leaders in the work of racial justice. A thousand clergy marched silently through the streets. Black pastors and clergy of color from various Christian traditions were followed by Protestants, Greek Orthodox, the Roman Catholic archbishop and Dominican priests, rabbis, imams, Buddhist monks, Unitarians, and others.

When the sounds of marching feet arrived at the sacred place where George Floyd had been killed, Bishop Richard D. Howell Jr. asked everyone to take a knee and together pray the Lord's Prayer. On our knees, we redeemed this space from the horror of former police officer Derek Chauvin's knee that killed George Floyd. Clergy and gathered community members prayed for God's will to be done on earth as it is in heaven.[17] The visual of a Black-led, faith-inspired multiracial march out of Egypt, out of George Floyd Square, signals the possibility of transformation.

In this moment, the words of South African anti-apartheid activist and theologian Russel Botman ring true. A few years prior to his untimely death, I was in conversation with him. He had been appointed the first Black rector and vice chancellor of the historically white Afrikaner University of Stellenbosch in South Africa. His continued work for racial justice was premised on one central motive: "in the interest of future generations." He clarified, "If we do not get it right, future generations will judge this as a missed opportunity as they will carry the burden."[18] Out of George Floyd Square, God has called us to transformation. If we do not get it right, future generations will judge this as a missed opportunity. And they will have to carry the burden.

Hold on to the word *transformation*.

Out of Egypt, out of Africa, out of George Floyd Square, we are being called to liberation, affirmation, and transformation. We must not miss this opportunity!

Notes

1. Raymond E. Brown, *The Birth of the Messiah: A Commentary on the Infancy Narratives in Matthew and Luke* (Garden City, NY: Image Books, 1979), 203.

2. R. T. France, *The Gospel of Matthew* (Grand Rapids, MI: Eerdmans, 2007), 79.

3. Ibid., 84–85.

4. It was common for Bibles to have pictures of biblical characters all portrayed as white Europeans. A few recent Bibles have attempted to counter this. See Cain Hope Felder, ed., *The Original African Heritage Study Bible* (Valley Forge, PA: Judson Press, 2007); Curtiss Paul DeYoung, Wilda C. Gafney, Leticia A. Guardiola-Sáenz, George ("Tink") Tinker, and Frank M. Yamada, eds. *The Peoples' Bible: New Revised Standard Version with Apocrypha* (Minneapolis: Fortress, 2008).

5. Frank Madison Reid III, "Jesus Had an African Connection," Bethel African Methodist Episcopal Church (Baltimore, MD), December 1, 1996, audiocassette.

6. *First Nations Version: An Indigenous Translation of the New Testament* (Downers Grove, IL: InterVarsity Press, 2021), 3.

7. Felder, *The Original African Heritage Study Bible*, 4–5.

8. Rodney S. Sadler Jr. "Genesis," in *The Africana Bible: Reading Israel's Scriptures from Africa and the African Diaspora*, Hugh R. Page Jr., gen. ed. (Minneapolis: Fortress, 2010), 73; Cain Hope Felder, "Race, Racism, and the Biblical Narratives," in *Stony the Road We Trod: African American Biblical Interpretation—Thirtieth Anniversary Expanded Edition*, ed. Cain Hope Felder (Minneapolis: Fortress, 2021), 148–51; Gene Rice, *Africa and the Bible:*

Corrective Lenses (Eugene, OR: Cascade Books, 2019), 91–104.

9. Charles B. Copher, *Black Biblical Studies: An Anthology of Charles B. Copher* (Chicago: Black Light Fellowship, 1993), 135.

10. Cain Hope Felder, *Troubling Biblical Waters: Race, Class, and Family* (Maryknoll, NY: Orbis Books, 1989), 37; Curtiss Paul DeYoung, *Coming Together in the Twenty-First Century: The Bible's Message in an Age of Diversity* (Valley Forge, PA: Judson Press, 2009), 53–54.

11. This scholarship is included and cited in DeYoung, *Coming Together in the Twenty-First Century.*

12. The full story of this event in South Africa is detailed in Curtiss Paul DeYoung, *Homecoming: A "White" Man's Journey through Harlem to Jerusalem* (Eugene, OR: Wipf & Stock, 2009, 2015), 99–111.

13. France, 78.

14. "What Hollywood Keeps Getting Wrong about Race," The Daily, February 26, 2019, www.nytimes.com/2019/02/26/podcasts/the-daily/oscars-green-book-interracial-friendship.html.

15. Alexis Allston, "Mural Raises Concerns about Representation in Art Responding to George Floyd's Killing," *StarTribune*, July 8, 2020, www.startribune.com/mural-raises-concerns-about-representation-in-art-after-george-floyd-s-killing/571660341.

16. Tour of George Floyd Square by Rev. Jeanelle Austin, January 3, 2022.

17. The Silent Clergy march on June 2, 2020, was the vision of Presiding Elder Stacey L. Smith of the St. Paul Minneapolis District of the African Methodist Episcopal Church. She was joined by several other Black clergy in the planning and leadership of the march. Bishop Richard D. Howell Jr. of the Pentecostal Assemblies of the World and senior pastor of Shiloh Temple International Ministries led the Lord's Prayer at George Floyd Square. Shiloh Temple would later host the funerals of Daunte Wright and Amir Locke.

18. Russel Botman, quoted in DeYoung, *Homecoming*, 146.

SECTION 2

The Call to Community
Jesus Defines Family at the Cross

Near the cross of Jesus stood his mother, his mother's sister, Mary the wife of Clopas, and Mary Magdalene. When Jesus saw his mother there, and the disciple whom he loved standing nearby, he said to his mother, "Dear woman, here is your son," and to the disciple, "Here is your mother." From that time on, this disciple took her into his home. (John 19:25-27, NIV)

The public liturgy of the empire's power began as the four-man execution squad nailed Jesus of Nazareth to a cross (John 19:23). All eyes were fastened on (or perhaps fascinated by) the frenzy of state-sanctioned ritual degradation and horrific slaughter called crucifixion. In May 2020, ten blocks from my house and four blocks from my church, a four-man execution squad of Minneapolis police publicly performed an execution with a knee on the neck of George Perry Floyd Jr. Nearly two thousand years separate these two state-sanctioned killings of marginalized, oppressed persons with African ancestry.

The four-man execution squad was not the only story that day in Jerusalem. Off to the side were four women who offered a counter witness and told a story different from what was being told about the killing of Jesus by the Roman Empire.[1] Four women, not the four executioners, defined the story in John's Gospel. While the four-man execution squad commanded the public drama, four women—and the disciple whom Jesus loved—took center stage in the Gospel's telling.

At the cross, Jesus looks for his mother. As George Floyd was dying, he called for his mother. As we approach our last breath of life, we seem to be drawn to the one who gave us our first breath of life. When we heard the recorded voice of George Floyd calling for his mother, we recognized our shared humanity. John preserved for us in his Gospel a powerfully poignant moment. Amid the drama of crucifixion on a day that altered history, John inserted a poetic pause so that readers might gain a glimpse into a very human encounter between a dying son and his grieving mother in the presence of their extended family. His execution could not diminish his humanity.

Crucified persons were often surrounded by family. Jesus' mother, Mary, was there. The sister of Jesus' mother was there. In the other Gospels, she was called Salome or the mother of the sons of Zebedee.[2] She was Jesus' aunt. The sons of Zebedee were Jesus' disciples James and John. Therefore, the disciple whom Jesus loved, John, was the son of the sister of Jesus' mother.[3] John was Mary's nephew and Jesus' cousin. Interestingly, in the Gospel of John, none of Jesus' biological relatives were called by their names. They were referred to as mother, sister, disciple whom Jesus loved.

The third woman was Mary, the wife of Clopas. This is the only time she was mentioned in the Bible. Second-century historian Eusebius wrote that Clopas was the brother of Joseph (the husband of Mary, Jesus' mother). That would mean that she was the sister-in-law of Jesus' mother—another aunt of Jesus.[4] The fourth woman was Mary Magdalene.[5] She was not a family member but was included in the family circle. With Mary Magdalene, the line between family and friends became blurred.

Crucified men had the right to make legal dispositions from the cross.[6] Also, the eldest son bore the religious duty and cultural expectation to care for his widowed mother. So as Jesus was in the process of dying, he addressed the care of his mother and what her legal status would be after his death. Jesus said to his mother, "Here is your son." And to John, "Here is your mother." He used formulaic language from ancient Jewish family law to transfer the care of his mother to his cousin and disciple John. The Gospel states that John took his aunt Mary into his home. All of this was witnessed by John's own mother, Salome.

Mary Magdalene did not have the obligation of family and kinship. While Mary Magdalene was included in this private family moment, she was not obligated or required to be there. This was a choice. Mary Magdalene had lived her entire life under the occupation of Rome. She was way too familiar with crucifixion—Rome's method for executing revolutionaries. She was devoted to Jesus even though she saw no hope. She was loyal to Jesus without the knowledge of Easter coming. Mary had a deep commitment that was not dependent on external factors. We don't have to be family to be faithful. But if we are faithful, we become family. Mary Magdalene models for us the central notion of community.

The site of the killing of George Floyd in Minneapolis, now called George Floyd Square, hosted the first rally and protest the day after his death. From that first day on May 26, 2020, people have shown up and tended to memories, rage, and grief, and stood up against racial injustice. Among those gathering were Floyd's family members. But many others, unrelated by blood, have become family through faithfulness.

At the cross, Jesus curates the formation of a new family defined by faith community when "the claims of this family outweigh biological claims."[7] The lines between family and friends become blurred in this new community. Section 2 highlights the importance of community in the work of racial justice. This section focuses on healing community when it becomes dysfunctional, skills for building community, and sustaining community as God's way toward justice.

Notes

1. The NRSV implies there are three women. The NIV suggests four women. The Greek syntax is unclear. Most scholars prefer four women. The contrast between four soldiers and four women also lends support for this conclusion.

2. See Raymond E. Brown, *The Gospel According to John, XIII–XXI*, Anchor Yale Bible (New Haven, CT: Yale University Press, 1970), 905; G. R. Beasley-Murray, *John*, Word Biblical Commentary 36 (Waco, TX: Word Books, 1987), 348.

3. For arguments about the identity of the disciple whom Jesus loved and preference for the apostle John as that disciple, see Raymond E. Brown, *The Gospel According to John, I–XII*, Anchor Bible (Garden City, NY: Doubleday, 1966), xcii–xcviii.

4. Brown, *John XIII–XXI*, 906.

5. The name Magdalene is often thought to refer to Magdala as her place of origin. Some recent scholars are challenging this assumption: "Magdalene may well be an honorific from the Hebrew and Aramaic roots for tower or magnified. Just as Peter was given the epithet rock, Mary could well have acquired a title meaning tower of faith or Mary the magnified." See Yonat Shimron, "Was Mary Magdalene Really from Magdala? Two Scholars Examine the Evidence," *Christian Century* (February 9, 2022), 16.

6. Beasley-Murray, 349.

7. Marianne Meye Thompson, *John: A Commentary* (Louisville, KY: Westminster John Knox, 2015), 400.

CHAPTER 8

The In-between Time

He gave them this command: "Do not leave Jerusalem, but wait for the gift my Father promised." . . . Then they returned to Jerusalem from the hill called the Mount of Olives, a Sabbath's day walk from the city. When they arrived, they went upstairs to the room where they were staying. Those present were Peter, John, James and Andrew; Philip and Thomas, Bartholomew and Matthew; James son of Alphaeus, and Simon the Zealot, and Judas son of James.

They all joined together constantly in prayer, along with the women and Mary the mother of Jesus, and with his brothers. . . . Therefore, it is necessary to choose one of those who have been with us the whole time the Lord Jesus went in and out among us.

(Acts 1:4, 12-14, 21, NIV)

The closure of Jesus' earthly ministry opened a new season where his followers would become "witnesses in Jerusalem, and in all Judea and Samaria, and to the ends of the earth" (Acts 1:8, NIV). Theologian Willie Jennings suggests that these followers of Jesus would "be turned out to the world not as representatives of empires but those who will announce a revolution [entering] new places to become new people by joining themselves to those in Judea, Samaria, and the ends of the Earth."[1] The opening lines of

Acts narrate a transition that occurred as Jesus ascended into heaven and his followers faced the challenge of carrying on as a faith community without their leader. This was an in-between time—the time between what was and what was yet to come. The in-between time is after what has happened and before what is yet to happen. It is the time between before and after. Before was when Jesus lived, died, was resurrected, and ascended. After would come with Pentecost, the expansion of the first-century church, and, as Jennings declares, the announcement of a revolution.

Our text describes what happened between the three years of Jesus' ministry and the launch of the first-century church at Pentecost. We do not always have the benefit of an in-between time. For example, when one's town is struck by a disaster like a tornado or an earthquake, everything changes in an instant. When a loved one dies in a car accident, our personal lives are abruptly disrupted. The United States was dramatically transformed by a terrorist attack on September 11, 2001. Life in the United States was immediately and forever altered.

Yet, we are familiar with the in-between time. Our life cycles often have such a rhythm. We have no children. Then we get pregnant and enter a nine-month in-between time. Or we seek to adopt. The wait for the arrival of our new child is an in-between time. This is followed by parenthood. Sometimes we intentionally choose to create some space in our lives. Graduating high school students take a gap year prior to starting college. Some in-between times last longer than nine months or a year. Nelson Mandela led the revolution against apartheid in South Africa. He was imprisoned at age forty-four. He spent twenty-seven years in prison, which became a transformative in-between time. The revolutionary activist left prison at age seventy-one to become the reconciler president of the nation. (More about Mandela's in-between time later.)

The onset of COVID-19 created a global pause that many embraced as an in-between time. The slowdown of life served as a moment for reassessing life goals, career ambitions, relational commitments, and lifestyle practices. Many businesses, organizations, and faith communities reconsidered their ways of operating. Combined with the killing of George Floyd, the pandemic opened a space for increased racial reckoning. Also, many in the world woke up to the ominous reality of global climate change.

Our text describes an in-between time: after Jesus ascended and before Pentecost. Embracing transitions helps ensure that communities continue to exist and thrive. The community founded by Jesus faced the departure of its leader. Their desire to hold onto the past limited their ability to step into the future. They needed healing due to the unaddressed damage done by Judas's betrayal. In times of transition, faith communities and activist organizations can face unexamined leadership issues, dysfunctional or toxic culture, disappointment at the failure to fully achieve goals, and the like. This reflection calls for creating space to address these very real challenges to the health of a community before embracing new opportunities.

Do Not Leave Jerusalem

Jesus commanded his followers, "Do not leave Jerusalem" (Acts 1:4, NIV). After Jesus ascended into heaven, his followers traveled to Jerusalem where they were staying in an upper room. They were not to leave Jerusalem, the "city built with the bricks of prophecy."[2] Jesus told his disciples to stay in Jerusalem because the interim between his leaving and the coming of the Holy Spirit was an important moment to prepare for the future that awaited them. There was prophetic wisdom waiting for them. Great value and insight can be discovered during the in-between time. We must not miss the gifts of the in-between time. We must not waste the interim moments in our lives.

I moved to Minneapolis fresh from seminary as a new pastor of a local church. After serving for nearly five years, I was burned out and left the church with no certain permanent job on the horizon. My seminary mentor, Cain Hope Felder, suggested that this might be a moment of great creativity. It was a time of uncertainty and meager finances. Yet, Dr. Felder was right. I had felt called to a ministry of reconciliation and racial justice. I left pastoral ministry broken and burned out. I believed that the flame of my calling was extinguished. During a year of going from project to project in what became an in-between time, God began to fan the small flicker that remained and returned it to a burning fire. I learned to trust God for my financial situation. More so, I learned to first trust God with my calling. I personally know the importance and value of an in-between time.

Even though Jesus commanded his disciples to stay in Jerusalem for a season, they seemed to initially miss the importance of this in-between time. The next time they were together with Jesus they wanted to talk politics. "Lord, are you at this time going to restore the kingdom to Israel?" (Acts 1:6, NIV). Jesus had told them to go to Jerusalem and not leave. Sometimes we do not appreciate and value the pauses in our lives. Often, gifts waiting for us from God can be discovered only if we slow down and open our eyes, minds, and hearts.

After Jesus re-emphasized the need to stay in Jerusalem, he ascended into heaven and brought closure to his earthly days (Acts 1:9). The in-between time officially began. What was before had ended, but what was to come had not yet commenced. Given how insistent Jesus was that his disciples go to Jerusalem, you would expect they would hurry on their way to the Holy City. Rather, they stood "looking intently up into the sky" (1:10, NIV). They were still focused on the past. They did not want to let go. They did not feel ready to move on. This is normal. It becomes problematic if we get stuck in the past . . . if we are obsessed with the before. Angelic messengers came along and helped the disciples disengage from the before and move on into the in-between time (1:10-11).

Sometimes, we need a heavenly visitor to stop by and help us move forward into the transition.

Before we leave these first words about the importance of the in-between time, I also want to say that equally problematic is the temptation to move immediately to the future. Again, this is a normal desire. We are often advised not to look back and move quickly into the next phase. If we place all our focus on what is next, the after, then we also miss the gift of the in-between time. Often this interim time holds the key that unlocks the future that God desires for us. We must not leave Jerusalem. We can learn much from this biblical pause, this sacred space, this redemptive rupture in history.

Wait for the Gift

Jesus told his disciples to wait for the gift that was promised. So, they joined together in prayer. Waiting meant prayer, contemplation, and reflection. I think it also meant rest and healing. The prophet Isaiah hinted at what waiting could bring: "Those who wait for the Lord shall renew their strength; they shall mount up with wings like eagles; they shall run and not be weary, they shall walk and not faint" (40:31).

Nelson Mandela waited for twenty-seven years in prison for the fullness of the gift that would come from his in-between time. In the early 1970s, while in prison on Robben Island, Nelson Mandela planted a garden. This became his spiritual discipline for waiting. It took some time to gain the permission of the prison authorities. Finally, they acceded to his request to grow some vegetables in the hard and rocky ground. He was given a small part of the dismal courtyard in front of the prisoners' cells. His family sent him seeds. At first, prison officials were suspicious of Mandela's motives. But he continued to tend to his garden providing vegetables to the kitchen to improve the diet of prisoners. Over time, he was allowed to expand his garden, and he even shared the produce with the guards and their families. As Mandela biographer Richard Stengel notes, "On Robben Island, where there were few pleasures, Mandela's garden had become his own private island. It quieted his mind. It distracted him from his constant worries about the outside world, his family, and the freedom struggle. . . . In a world that he could not control, that defied and punished him, that seemed hostile to his values and his dreams, it had been a place of beauty and regularity and renewal."[3] His fellow freedom fighter and prisoner Ahmed Kathrada said, "He loved that garden."[4] Later, Mandela advised others, "You must find your own garden."[5]

Jesus had his Garden of Gethsemane. Nelson Mandela had his garden on the prison grounds of Robben Island. We must find or create our own garden. Jesus' advice to stay in Jerusalem and wait for the gift was not meant to be done only in the solitude of a garden. Jesus told his followers to spend their time in Jerusalem with each other: the Eleven, the women, and the family of Jesus (Acts 1:13). A portion of the gift waiting for them was to deepen their formation of community through prayer, fellowship, and caring for each other after the trauma and triumph of crucifixion and resurrection. Their community blended the biological and spiritual family. The in-between time has an important communal dimension.

It Is Necessary

The names listed in our text reminded the readers that there remained only eleven of "the twelve" disciples who followed Jesus throughout Palestine (Acts 1:13). Jesus' choice of twelve disciples was a symbolic reflection of the twelve tribes of Israel. It seemed important to move into the future in a way that was consistent with the past. Peter felt that it was "necessary" to address what had happened (1:21, NIV). They replaced Judas with Matthias (1:21-26). Perhaps it was even more important to repair the wrong committed against the community of Jesus' followers by Judas's betrayal. As Peter said of Judas, "he was one of our number and shared in this ministry" (1:17, NIV). Judas had inflicted a deep wound on the community. He had been chosen by Jesus, trusted by the others, and yet, he betrayed them all. I think Peter's graphic description of Judas's death was meant as a pictorial representation of how his actions were experienced by the community of believers: "He fell headlong, his body burst open and all his intestines spilled out" (1:18, NIV).

The in-between time provides us with the opportunity to address the messiness in our own lives and our families, and in our communities. This pause offers us space to resolve issues and challenges left undone from the past, so we do not drag them with us into the future. The in-between time prepares us "for an unknown future, aware of a troubled past."[6] Peter was right; it was necessary. Perhaps it was a strategic choice by Jesus not to deal with the aftermath of Judas's betrayal before he left. The community needed to grapple with this themselves. Peter felt it was necessary to deal with this lingering issue before the next phase of their community journey commenced. The in-between time is an amazing gift that enables us to ready ourselves for God's desired future. We can address unresolved issues. We can clean up emotional messes and detox our relationships. We can carefully reflect on our strategies for the future. We can grow and develop as individuals and communities so that we are ready for the next phase.

While in prison, Nelson Mandela organized an ad hoc university, developed policy for an African National Congress–led government, envisioned strategies for ruling the country, and embraced his own growth as a leader. Stengel reflects, "Nelson Mandela had many teachers in his life, but the greatest of them all was prison. . . . The Nelson Mandela who emerged from prison at seventy-one was a different man from the Nelson Mandela who went in at forty-four."[7] Prior to prison, Mandela was described by friend and fellow freedom fighter Oliver Tambo this way: "As a man,

Nelson Mandela is passionate, emotional, sensitive, quickly stung to bitterness and retaliation by insult and patronage."[8] Stengel pensively asked, "How did this passionate revolutionary become a measured statesman?"[9] He repeatedly asked Mandela, "How was the man who came out in 1990 different from the man who entered in 1962?" Finally, one day, tired of the question, Mandela blurted out, "I came out mature."[10]

The in-between time offers us the opportunity to mature, to develop, to grow in wisdom, to be ready for the next phase in life. His time in prison prepared Nelson Mandela to be the president of a new South Africa. The anti-apartheid struggle of the 1960s needed the revolutionary Mandela. The nation-building of the 1990s South Africa needed the reconciler Mandela. The in-between time on Robben Island also matured the larger community of revolutionaries and prepared them to serve with Mandela in transforming South Africa.

When Peter said, "it is necessary," he was reminding us that the in-between time is a unique opportunity to address unresolved issues that we should not carry into the next phase of our lives, make important plans for the future during this pause in life, and grow and develop in ways needed in order to be successful in the next phase. We can become mature people. Like Mandela, Peter needed to mature. The impulsive disciple who denied three times knowing Jesus became the apostolic leader and Pentecost preacher. And it is necessary for communities to mature, to become healthy, and to strategize for the future during the in-between time.

Pentecost

Eventually, the season of in-between ends, and we move into the time after. For the disciples of Jesus, that occurred on the day of Pentecost. "When the day of Pentecost came, they were all together in one place" (Acts 2:1, NIV). They were ready to boldly lead the launch of the first-century church—the new community of followers of Jesus. We must embrace the in-between time when it comes. We will be prepared as leaders and communities to boldly step into what is next if we do not leave Jerusalem, if we wait for the gift, and if we address what is necessary.

Notes

1. Willie James Jennings, *Acts* (Louisville, KY: Westminster John Knox, 2017), 18.

2. Robert W. Wall, "The Acts of the Apostles," *The New Interpreter's Bible* 10, ed. Leander E. Keck (Nashville: Abingdon, 2002), 41.

3. Richard Stengel, *Mandela's Way: Fifteen Lessons on Life, Love, and Courage* (New York: Crown, 2009), 220, 223.

4. Ibid., 221.

5. Ibid., 224.

6. Jennings, 24.

7. Stengel, 14.

8. Ibid., 15.

9. Ibid.

10. Ibid., 17.

CHAPTER 9

Sameness Meets Creoleness

Now the whole earth had one language and the same words. (Genesis 11:1)

When the day of Pentecost had come, they were all together in one place. And suddenly from heaven there came a sound like the rush of a violent wind, and it filled the entire house where they were sitting. Divided tongues, as of fire, appeared among them, and a tongue rested on each of them. All of them were filled with the Holy Spirit and began to speak other languages, as the Spirit gave them ability. Now there were devout Jews from every nation under heaven living in Jerusalem. . . . in our own languages we hear them speaking about God's deeds of power. (Acts 2:1-5, 11)

The Fatal Attraction of Sameness

In the eleventh chapter of Genesis, we encounter the story traditionally called "the Tower of Babel." The author of Genesis shared origin stories in the first ten chapters. Then, in chapter 11, the origin of human cultural and linguistic diversity was described. The chapter begins with the statement that the entire planet had only one language. All human beings spoke the same language using the same words with the same accent. "One language" is more literally translated "one lip."[1] This was such a different world than today where we have multiple languages. We even have multiple ways to speak the same language, including different accents or pronunciations. In the same language, words may have different meanings depending on the place where spoken. I learned in South Africa that the trunk of a car is called the boot, a traffic light is called a robot, and a diaper is called a napkin. When someone from the United States refers to wiping their face with a napkin, South Africans respond with disgust.

We are told in Genesis 11 that humanity was seeking sameness. The human family wanted one culture, one language, "one lip." In the first ten chapters of Genesis, God told the human family to "fill the earth" and to scatter (Genesis 1:28; 9:1). Such a geographic scattering would create cultural and language diversity. To avoid being "scattered abroad upon the face of the whole earth," they built a tower to "make a name" for themselves (11:4). The tower was likely a Babylonian ziggurat, "a temple-tower presented as an imperial embodiment of pride and self-sufficiency."[2]

Also, they were no longer talking to God, but rather only to each other. Adam and Eve, Cain, and Noah all conversed with God. In Genesis 11, the human family was ignoring God and departing from God's will for the human family to become diverse. Theologian Miguel De La Torre calls this a "rebellion . . . rooted in an arrogance of power, where political and economic order become ends in themselves."[3] They were building a city with a tower, which made a name for themselves rather than a name for God. They found unity in sameness and safety in homogeneity. They sought a self-made and self-centered identity, separate from God. Is this the first biblical sighting of the human family attempting to build an empire? This desire—this tendency—rings true to the challenges of our own time as we "struggle with our own colonial appetites."[4] Unity as sameness is the core of white nationalism, Nazi allegiance, and anti-immigrant or anti-refugee sentiment.

Biblical scholar Theodore Hiebert suggests an alternate view of what was happening at Babel. He contends that the human family was doing the things that make us human with a common culture: "language, land, and name." Hiebert notes that this was humanity's fresh start after the end of the flood navigated by Noah. It was an attempt to build "their own unique, esteemed, and lasting identity in the world."[5] While Hiebert's view has merit, the author of Genesis stressed the point that the human family was actively seeking not to scatter—avoiding God's will—and only talking among themselves and not with God. They had a clear objective to maintain a sense of sameness. Even if we find De La Torre's warning of empire building too drastic, I suggest an exclusive focus on sameness can lead to the same outcome. What we observe in our text is the story of culture building without God. Build a tower. Unify around sameness. Secure a secular future without God in defiance of God's desire for diversity. Reap the results of the fatal attraction of sameness. Sameness is toxic.

God Interrupts Sameness

Even though the human family had departed from God's vision for the human community, the Almighty stayed nearby and in relationship. This is an important truth. God is always nearby. So, God initiated an intervention. "The LORD came down to see the city and the tower, which mortals had built" (Genesis 11:5). Many believed that God only dwelled in the heavens. The Genesis story had God travel to Earth to learn what was going on. Obviously, it was not a tower that extended into the heavens if God had to come down to see it. The biblical narrator clearly pointed out the difference between the Divine and humanity by using the term "mortals" (Hebrew *benei ha-'adam*), which emphasized human frailty in comparison with God's limitless power and presence.[6] The finite had dismissed the desire of the Infinite.

God called out and exposed the fatal flaw of unity built on sameness. "Look, they are one people, and they have all one language; and this is only the beginning of what they will do; nothing that they propose to do will now be impossible for them" (Genesis 11:6). The fatal attraction of sameness can produce the toxic consequences of racism, sexism, classism, heterosexism, white nationalism, apartheid, slavery, genocide, and ethnic cleansing. Bow down to Babel and embrace the fatal attraction of sameness or stand up with God.

God Desires Diversity, Inclusion, Equity

The Genesis author continued, "'Come, let us go down, and confuse their language there, so that they will not understand one another's speech.' So the LORD scattered them abroad from there over the face of all the earth, and they left off building the city. Therefore it was called Babel, because there the LORD confused the language of all the earth" (Genesis 11:7-9). God confused their language. Hiebert prefers to translate the Hebrew word *balal* as "mix" rather than "confuse."[7] God mixed their language. God's scattering of the human family was an act of grace! God blocked tower building and name making. God blocked a cultural context that could lead to imperialism, colonialism, and nationalism. God blocked sameness. While scattering might have appeared as punishment, it was a redirection toward God's will. It was living into God's purpose for humanity. God's desire was diversity.

The narrative of Genesis 11 closed with the arrival of Abraham, who became the progenitor of the portion of the scattered human family whose story was told in the pages of the Hebrew Scriptures—and later appeared in the New Testament and the Quran. With the arrival of Abraham, a relationship with and primary identity in God returned to the human family. Through the descendants of his wives, Sarah and Hagar, came many nations, languages, and three religions. Genesis 11 ended with the promise of God's desire for diversity through Abraham and the many others whose stories are not recorded.

As a Christian preacher, I am drawn to the New Testament event that is called the completion of Babel. I am speaking of Pentecost (Acts 2). The story of the tower of Babel in Genesis 11 ended with the promise of diversity through Abraham and the scattering of humanity. The scattering created a multiplicity of languages and cultures. Hiebert's translation of *balal* as "mixing" is intriguing. It is as though the author of Genesis inserted a forethought of Pentecost theology. Pentecost was certainly a mixing of languages and cultures. Today, we could call Pentecost a creolizing moment. Creolization is mixing or blending—a hybridization—both linguistically and culturally.[8]

The process of creolization is a helpful metaphor for understanding what happened at Pentecost and subsequent events in Acts. Creole is a human mixing of race, culture, and language. Creolization occurs in contexts of oppression, colonization, and slavery. The creolization process "is a response to oppression and colonization that has great potential to restore identity and engender self-acceptance, heal and humanize individuals and communities, and revolutionize societies."[9] Pentecost erupted in the context of the oppressive, colonial, slave-holding regime of the Roman Empire. Pentecost was an explosive Creole-like moment.

Before we wander too far into an idealized creolized community rooted in diversity, inclusion, and equity, let us pause as theologian Justo González warns us that many multicultural societies of today are "the result of European conquest and westward expansion." He continues, "It is the result of Black slavery and the trade that supported it. It is the result of colonialism in the nineteenth century, and of economic neocolonialism in the twentieth. It is the result of two world wars and a cold one. It is the result of civil wars in Central America, fostered by the great superpowers." We could add the attempted destruction and elimination of Indigenous peoples and cultures. González expressed his concern:

> Thus, when we look at our present-day communities and see them as multicultural, multiethnic microcosms in which all the nations, cultures, languages, and people of the world meet, it is important to realize that these communities are also the result of the vast forces, mostly evil forces, that have uprooted people and tossed them upon distant shores. A multiethnic society is a microcosm, not only of ethnic diversity throughout the world but also of the strife, injustice, and oppression that rule the world.[10]

Similarly, the first-century Jesus-inspired faith communities emerged in the heart of Roman colonial enterprise and expansionist exploits that contained, as González warns, "the strife, injustice and oppression that rule the world." As we examine the biblical text and apply it to today, we keep González's warning front and center. In biblical times and today, people have competing visions of what is authentic inclusion and equity in diverse communities. Yet, embedded in these Pentecost stories are some principles for creating and nurturing communities that embrace a motif of diversity, inclusion, and equity.

Embrace Diversity—Speak the Language of Someone Else's Experience

The Pentecost festival attracted Jews who had relocated to Jerusalem from all across the Roman Empire. While we might assume that all Jews spoke Hebrew or Aramaic, many from the diaspora spoke Greek, attended synagogues for Greek speakers, and read the Scriptures from a Greek translation called the

Septuagint.[11] The diversity of Jewishness from all cultural and linguistic contexts was on full display during Pentecost.

In Genesis 11:7, God confused or mixed language so that humans could no longer understand each other. They could no longer hear each other. Therefore, they no longer listened to each other.[12] Pentecost was about hearing each other. It was about "a fresh capacity to listen."[13] The author of Acts recorded this moment: "Each one heard them speaking in the native language of each. . . . How is it that we hear, each of us, in our own native language?" (2:6, 8). Biblical scholar Virginia Burrus remarks about Pentecost, "The disciples find not their own but 'other' hot languages in their mouths."[14] The disciples opened their mouths, and someone else's language and dialect came out replacing their own language. This was not a scene from *Star Trek* where beings from another world inhabit your body and use your vocal cords to communicate their message. When the disciples opened their mouths and another language came out, they were still themselves. They uttered these other languages with their Galilean accents displaying their regional origins. "Are not all these who are speaking Galileans?" (2:7).

Similarly, cultural competency is achieved when we understand the experience of another while still rooted in our own cultural reality. At Pentecost, the wind was heard before "a tongue rested on each of them" (2:3). Hearing came before speaking. We are better able to navigate diverse contexts as we learn to speak the language of other people's experiences. We first listen to their stories and observe their ways of living. Multicultural church pastor Jacqueline Lewis writes that we "need the capacity to be multivocal."[15] Multivocal capacity emerges from deep intentional listening.

As a student at Howard University School of Divinity, I became acquainted with Black liberation theology. Samuel Hines, my pastor at the Third Street Church of God in

Washington, DC, was not yet convinced about Black theology. When we discussed the matter, it created an unusual visual. I was a white man raised in white suburbs trying to persuade my Black pastor to consider Black liberation theology. The words that came out of my mouth were those of my Howard University theology professors. Another language was heard coming out of my mouth. The words spoken did not match my cultural origins, theological background, or racial look. My Pentecost moment demonstrated my growing competency in the ways of thinking and understanding in my new social location at a historically Black divinity school.

Embrace Inclusion—Speaking Simultaneously and Collectively

In addition to mixing diversity, Pentecost added inclusion. Inclusion occurred as Galilean Jewish followers of Jesus shouted in assorted languages that were not their own mother tongue. People from the continents of Asia, Africa, and Europe who lived in Jerusalem and attended the Pentecost feast heard these proclamations in the local languages and regional dialects of their countries of origin. Converts to Judaism from the capital city of Rome were also present, as well as Cretans and Arabs. They heard in their own languages. Even Roman soldiers on alert at the edges of the crowd, poised to exert measures of imperial control, were hearing in Latin, their own language (2:5, 9-11). We feel included when we hear our own language welcoming us.

The first thing this Pentecost story reminds us of is that we can learn to speak the language of someone else's experience. Second, we see in this text that they all participated, and all spoke these other languages simultaneously and collectively. "They were all together in one place. . . . All of them were filled with the Holy Spirit and began to speak" (2:1,4). Peter used the words of the

Hebrew prophet Joel to describe what happened that day (2:17-18; Joel 2:28-29). Peter in essence said that women and men, young and old, and even people who were enslaved by Rome could all speak in other languages. Pentecost speaking was inclusive. All could speak. All could hear. All participated.

I experienced this communal multivocal capacity when I first visited South Africa. I attended a ministry conference that was rare at the time for South Africa because people were gathered across all of the proscribed lines of race and all expressions of culture. The worship that occurred was a highly inclusive, fully participatory, simultaneous, and collective multicultural experience. The worship leaders blended various Black Indigenous African musical forms with aspects from other racial groups whose music was influenced by jazz emanating out of Coloured (Khoisan and mixed-race people) communities or contemporary praise music from Europe and the United States. Worship songs were sung in multiple languages while merging diverse cultural musical expressions. Each song was sung in its original language yet included verses in three or more additional languages (among the eleven official languages of South Africa). Dance was also an important part of the worship experience. As the musicians and singers transitioned from one language, cultural sound, and rhythm to the next, I was mesmerized by the synchronized and effortless shift by the participants to the culturally related dance moves. It was a musical mosaic of cultural competency.

At Pentecost "each one heard them speaking in the native language of each . . . How is it that we hear, each of us, in our own native language?" (2:6, 8). We discover and grow in our communal cultural competency when we learn to listen to and speak from each other's life experiences. Initially inclusion needs to be intentional or even directed. It may feel awkward and not come naturally. Over time, the experience of inclusion becomes a positive habit, both enriching and empowering.

Embrace Equity—Pentecost Deconstructs Power and Creates Community

When diverse peoples are fully included, equity ensures that opportunity and power are balanced and shared. Equity efforts focus on adjusting, adapting, or changing systems of interaction. Equity was implemented through Pentecost-like events as power was deconstructed. On the day of Pentecost in Jerusalem, second-class Galilean Jews and diasporic Jews were thrust into leadership by the Spirit. Jerusalem was normally the domain of established priestly Jewish families (2:37-42). The Samaritan Pentecost created an inclusive equality between Jews and Samaritans, who were marginalized in Jewish society (8:4-25). When the Spirit came to the home of the Roman centurion Cornelius, oppressed Jews gained equal status with ruling-class Romans (10:1-48). When the Pentecost Spirit stepped outside of the Roman Empire, it created a shared faith between Philip, an oppressed Jew, and an Ethiopian finance minister from ancient Nubia, ruled by Queen Candice (8:26-39).

This Pentecost movement blended cultures and deconstructed power hierarchies, creating Creole-like communities that included Palestinian Jews, diaspora Jews, colonial Romans, Greeks, Arabs, Samaritans, Ethiopians, and on and on. These Pentecost events placed a Creole-like imprint upon the church from its inception and launched diverse, inclusive, Creole-like faith communities throughout the Roman Empire that addressed systemic inequities. The equity of first-century Christian faith communities was apparent when dominant-culture Romans and Greeks joined with oppressed Jews in Jewish homes where first-century congregations gathered. It was unheard of for Romans and Greeks to sit with a socially stigmatized and marginalized community. Furthermore, Jews were leaders in first-century churches. While Greeks and Romans dominated Jews in society, these power dynamics were reversed in first-century congregations.[16]

Many organizations are implementing diversity, equity, and inclusion (DEI) initiatives. The acronym DEI is now the common shorthand. These organizations have DEI trainings, DEI officers, and DEI strategic planning. The goal is to ensure that DEI is infused throughout all aspects of organizational life. DEI needs to be in the DNA of the organization. Pentecost implanted DEI into the first-century church's DNA. We need to ensure that DEI is embedded in the DNA of our contemporary faith communities and activist organizations.

Embrace a New Posture

Pentecost is for everyone. Pentecost is a communal experience. Yet, Pentecost can neither be contained in an individual's experience, nor in a communal experience. Pentecost flows over into the streets. The group of 120 found themselves swept out of their house and into the streets. It was the day of Pentecost—the festival of weeks—so the streets of Jerusalem were filled with the full diversity of Jews from across the known world, including converts to Judaism and Roman soldiers. It is not difficult to locate diverse spaces today. Sporting events, concerts, public schools, many churches, and even protests can attract a diversity of people. By contrast, creating spaces that are fully inclusive and sustainably equitable requires effort and strategic intentionality.

In Acts 2:2, the entire household was sitting as they received the Spirit. They were sitting as they heard the violent wind and began to speak in other languages. But in verse 14, there was a change in posture. The author of Acts noted that Peter and the leaders were standing. When it was time to act, there was a change in posture.[17] DEI is in the DNA of the church. It is time to stop sitting around with that knowledge. It is time to stop sitting around with that competency. It is time to stop sitting around with that transforming Pentecost power. We need to embrace a new posture. Stand up!

Embrace and unleash the diversity, inclusion, and equity embedded in Pentecost.

Notes

1. Gordan J. Wenham, *Genesis 1–15*, Word Biblical Commentary 1 (Grand Rapids, MI: Zondervan, 1987), 238.

2. Walter Brueggemann, *Genesis* (Atlanta: John Knox Press, 1982), 98.

3. Miguel A. De La Torre, *Genesis* (Louisville, KY: Westminster John Knox, 2011), 134.

4. Ibid., 135.

5. Theodore Hiebert, *The Beginning of Difference: Discovering Identity in God's Diverse World* (Nashville: Abingdon Press, 2019), 9.

6. Nahum M. Sarna, *Genesis*. The JPS Torah Commentary (Philadelphia: The Jewish Publication Society, 1989), 83.

7. Hiebert, 19.

8. See Cambridge Dictionary: https://dictionary.cambridge.org/dictionary/english/creolization. Also, Stuart Hall, "Créolité and the Process of Creolization," in Robin Cohen and Paola Toninto, eds., *The Creolization Reader: Studies in Mixes Identities and Cultures* (London: Routledge, 2010). 28, 29.

9. Curtiss Paul DeYoung, Jacqueline J. Lewis, Micky ScottBey Jones, Robyn Afrik, Sarah Thompson Nahar, Sindy Morales Garcia, and 'Iwalani Ka'ai, *Becoming Like Creoles: Living and Leading at the Intersections of Injustice, Culture, and Religion* (Minneapolis: Fortress, 2019), 6.

10. Justo L. González, *For the Healing of the Nations: The Book of Revelation in an Age of Cultural Conflict* (Maryknoll, NY: Orbis, 1999), 84–85.

11. Isaiah Sone, "Synagogue," in George Arthur Buttrick, ed., *The Interpreter's Dictionary of the Bible: An Illustrated Encyclopedia, R–Z* (Nashville: Abingdon Press, 1962), 478–479.

12. De La Torre, *Genesis*, 136.

13. Brueggemann, 104.

14. Virginia Burrus, "The Gospel of Luke and Acts of the Apostles," in *A Postcolonial Commentary on the New Testament Writings*, ed. Fernando F. Segovia and R. S. Sugurtharajah (London: T & T Clark, 2009), 147.

15. Jacqueline J. Lewis, *The Power of Stories: A Guide for Leading Multi-Racial and Multi-Cultural Congregations* (Nashville: Abingdon Press, 2008), 68.

16. DeYoung, et al., *Becoming Like Creoles*, 1–4.

17. Thanks to Bishop Timothy J. Clarke for this insight about the change in posture.

CHAPTER 10

We Are Better Together

After this I looked, and there was a great multitude that no one could count, from every nation, from all tribes and peoples and languages, standing before the throne and before the Lamb, robed in white, with palm branches in their hands. . . . Then one of the elders addressed me, saying, "Who are these, robed in white, and where have they come from?" I said to him, "Sir, you are the one that knows." Then he said to me, "These are they who have come out of the great ordeal; they have washed their robes and made them white in the blood of the Lamb. For this reason they are before the throne of God, and worship him day and night within his temple, and the one who is seated on the throne will shelter them. They will hunger no more, and thirst no more; the sun will not strike them, nor any scorching heat; for the Lamb at the center of the throne will be their shepherd, and he will guide them to springs of the water of life, and God will wipe away every tear from their eyes." (Revelation 7:9, 13-17)

When Rev. Billy Russell was the president of the Minnesota State National Baptist Convention, his theme for the convention was *We Are Better Together!* As I reflected on his theme—we are better together—I noticed that it resonates throughout the entire Bible, from Genesis to Revelation. The biblical story began with creation. On the sixth day, God created humanity. The first human was called Adam (the Hebrew word for human). At the end of the sixth day, God saw everything that had been made and declared it was very good. I can imagine God looking at Adam and saying, We are better together! It was not long until God decided that it was not good for Adam to be alone as the only member of the human family. So, God created Eve. I can imagine Adam looking at Eve and saying, We are better together!

Not everyone in the biblical story embraced the theme of togetherness. Cain killed his brother Abel and when confronted by God said, "Am I my brother's keeper?" (Genesis 4:9). Others only embraced the theme later in life or in particular circumstances. It was at Abraham's death that his sons Isaac and Ishmael came together to bury their father. Only then could they say, We are better together! It was not until late in their lives that Jacob and Esau reconciled and could say, We are better together!

There are so many stories . . . Elijah found Elisha, placed his mantle over Elisha's shoulders, and said, We are better together! Shadrach, Meshach, and Abednego were thrown into a fiery furnace by King Nebuchadnezzar. There appeared a fourth man who looked like a son of God. Shadrach, Meshach, and Abednego looked at the fourth man and said, We are better together! Naomi's husband and two sons died in Moab. She decided to return to her home in Judah. Her daughter-in-law Ruth determined to go with Naomi and said, We are better together!

This notion of togetherness is also evident throughout the New Testament. The fact that God takes on human flesh and comes to earth in Jesus—Emmanuel, God with us—is God's way of saying, We are better together! Jesus chose twelve disciples to do ministry. At Pentecost, people from all cultures came together to launch the church. The apostle Paul did his ministry in partnerships—Paul and Barnabas; Paul and Silas; Paul, Priscilla, and Aquila. The apostle Paul wrote, "There is no longer Jew or Greek there is no longer slave or free; there is no longer male and female, for all of you are one in Christ Jesus" (Galatians 3:28). We are better together!

In Revelation 7, we are given a heavenly vision of what we are better together looks like from the vantage point of eternity. Let us linger on this text to gain a deeper understanding of why togetherness is preferred. John the Revelator painted a compelling picture of a great multitude that "no one could count" (7:9). This great multitude was the fulfillment of the promise to Abraham of "offspring as numerous as the stars of heaven" (Genesis 22:17). The size of the crowd around the throne certainly was beyond the imagination of the small first-century Christian community. They came "from every nation, from all tribes and peoples and languages" (Revelation 7:9). The gathering once again fulfilled the promise to Abraham that he would be "the ancestor of a multitude of nations" but now creolized by Pentecost (Genesis 17:4; see also Acts 2:5-11). John repeated this inclusive refrain several times in Revelation to emphasize God's universal invitation to membership in the family of God. He never used the same order for the words of this litany to further emphasize that we all have equal access to citizenship in the realm of God. No one is more or less important than anyone else.

This multitude arrived in the heavenly regions from all nations, tribes, people, and languages. They arrived in the Eternal City having worn the garments of cultural uniqueness, earthly identifiers, and socially constructed categories. Yet we are told that this multicultural, multiracial, multiethnic, multilingual multitude was one even as they were also diverse. They stood before the throne wearing the blood-washed robes of unity and reconciliation.

They were set free from all suffering. This picture of eternity reminds us that some will have been liberated from the oppressive effects of racism, sexism, and classism. Others will be set free from the suffocating air of race, gender, and class privilege. The elder proclaimed, "They will hunger no more and thirst no more"

(Revelation 7:16; see also Isaiah 49:10). I think I can safely add: Never again will anyone experience prejudice or bigotry. Never again will anyone experience sexual harassment. Never again will anyone experience homophobia. Never again will anyone experience poverty. Never again will anyone experience the feeling of being an outsider. Never again will anyone experience racial profiling, discrimination, Jim Crow, hate crimes, lynching, genocide, and ethnic cleansing.

What a wonderful, inspiring, comforting, and captivating picture of real human community free from all injustice and pain! Somehow when read today, it seems idealistic, romantic, and naive. Yet for the first-century church, this heavenly photograph was similar to the reality occurring in their congregational life. The first-century church was formed out of Pentecost and the model of the Antioch congregation. Before John stepped onto the isle of Patmos and saw this vision, he and other first-century Christians were already experiencing diversity, inclusion, and equity in their congregations.

For a moment, let us leave John and the isle of Patmos and discover what preceded this heavenly vision. Let us trace the DNA of the first-century church. As we wander back through the apostolic letters and the Acts of the Apostles, we see the apostle Paul spend his final days in the imperial capital city of Rome. As we examine the names of people interacting with him alongside the names of people he greeted in his letter to the church in Rome, we see Latin names, Greek names, and Jewish names (Romans 16). Also, on the continent of Europe, congregations comprised of Jews, Greeks, and Romans emerged in Corinth, Thessalonica, and Philippi. Simultaneously and prior to expanding through Europe, Paul and his associates founded faith communities in Asia. Most notable was the congregation in Ephesus. The outreach to Asia and Europe was launched from the very diverse congregation in Antioch of Syria whose leadership team brought together people from Africa,

Asia, and Palestine. The first congregations were formed in Jerusalem and broader Palestine and included Jews, Samaritans, Greeks, and Romans.

This story of a diverse and reconciled faith community had already been spoken of by a resurrected Jesus: "But you will receive power when the Holy Spirit comes upon you, and you will be my witnesses in Jerusalem, in all Judea and Samaria, and to the ends of the earth" (Acts 1:8). Jesus had witnessed the powerful coming together when an African, Simon of Cyrene, carried his cross and a European, a Roman centurion, spoke words of faith at the crucifixion of Jesus. Jesus had spent three years drawing together a radically inclusive congregation of followers—Jews, Greeks, Samaritans; men and women, and people who were disabled. In his final public message in the temple, he quoted Isaiah: "My house shall be called a house of prayer for all the nations" (Mark 11:17; see also Isaiah 56:7).

Jesus was raised in Galilee of the Gentiles—a multicultural and multilingual region of Palestinian Jews, Africans, Asians, and Europeans. The Gospels began with the advent of Jesus arriving as a baby, worshipped by Palestinian shepherds and Asian Magi, and then fleeing as a refugee to Africa. From Jesus to the first-century church to the isle of Patmos, we witness the multicultural, multi-ethnic, multiracial, multilingual DNA of God's salvation story. From Matthew to Revelation, the New Testament witnessed the importance of togetherness. Revelation 7 takes us deeper to tell us something about the quality of our unity revealed in our diversity in Christ. Three points emerge from this text in Revelation that will help us discover this quality of togetherness in community.

First, we are better together when we share a faith focus. This diverse gathering of people was "standing before the throne and before the Lamb" (7:9). The Lamb is a reference to Jesus. In this heavenly assembly, each person was focused on Jesus. Jesus was the center—the primary focus of their existence. Our primary focus—that which determines our values and our decisions—cannot be our career ambitions, our political persuasions, our cultural backgrounds, or our family heritages. The message, ministry, and abiding presence of Jesus in our lives is primary—it must be first. Our primary focus is Jesus—not our job, our clothes, our car, or our home. Our primary focus is Jesus—not the Methodists, Catholics, Baptists, or any other denomination. Our primary focus is Jesus—not the Republicans, Democrats, Greens, Independents, or any other political party. Our primary focus is Jesus—not culture, family, or other affiliations. Our primary focus is Jesus—not the United States of America.

A song that reflects this notion is "Center of My Joy."[1] The song speaks to the centrality of Jesus. What is not often noted is that the song was co-written by Richard Smallwood, William Gaither, and Gloria Gaither. Smallwood is Black, and the Gaithers are white. Both represent stellar gospel music traditions. The writing of the song was a witness to how they were better together as they centered their focus on Jesus.

South African theologian and anti-apartheid activist Allan Boesak sums it up best as he often says, "The more I say justice, I have to say Jesus. The more I say Jesus, I will have to say justice."[2] This is so true as we seek to center racial justice action in our communities. At the center of focusing on Jesus is focusing on racial justice. The more we call for racial justice, the more we call for Jesus. The more we observe the ministry of Jesus, the more we see racial justice and equity. No justice, no Jesus.

Second, we are better together when we bear our troubles together with community. The people in this diverse group "are they who have come out of the great ordeal" (7:14). In this heavenly assembly, they are those who have persevered through crises, troubles, and tribulations together in community. When Revelation 7 was read for the first time by followers of Jesus, these words were a powerful encouragement. In the first-century world, Caesar was seen as an all-powerful god. The gospel of the Roman world was the good news that Caesar had established peace, albeit by military force. Caesar was believed to be the savior who brought salvation. When Christians claimed that Jesus brought the good news of salvation, they were in direct opposition to Caesar. When they read that the great multitude cried out, "Salvation belongs to our God who is seated on the throne and to the Lamb," they knew that they could persevere (7:10). They saw the future, and there was no Caesar!

The Roman Empire sustained its peace through domination and force. One of its deterrents to rebellion by those oppressed under the empire's rule was crucifixion. Seventy years before Jesus was born, six thousand followers of Spartacus were crucified in Rome. Crucifixion was used to break the will and spirit of conquered peoples. It was used extensively in Jerusalem. Around the time of Jesus' birth, two thousand Judean freedom fighters were crucified at once by the Roman general Varus. Later, the Roman general Titus crucified as many as five hundred a day during a siege of Jerusalem until there was no more room for crosses outside the city walls.[3] And the Romans crucified Jesus of Nazareth! The early followers of Jesus took that tool of repression—crucifixion—and turned it into a symbol of resistance. Every time early followers of Jesus preached about his crucifixion, they proclaimed that their loyalties were with the reign of God and not the empire of Rome. They announced that Jesus was their Lord and *not* Caesar; they reminded Rome that the empire did not have the final word. No, the final word was resurrection!

When early followers of Jesus read that "they have washed their robes . . . in the blood of the Lamb," they knew that God's resurrection power would help them persevere (7:14). When we persevere through the tribulation and troubles that come from placing our primary focus on Jesus and racial justice we bond together. The heavenly vision tells us that we must come together in community and help each other persevere in the face of tribulation.

A few years ago, I fell and severed my Achilles tendon. I fell backward carrying too heavy of a load down a flight of stairs in the back of the apartment where we lived in Chicago. I landed with the full weight of my body on my right ankle. I felt something snap and experienced incredible pain. I initially thought it was just a sprained ankle and did not immediately visit a doctor. Therefore, it was seven weeks before surgery occurred. My surgeon warned me that surgery could be problematic because I had seven weeks of scar tissue built up. When I came out of surgery, the surgeon informed me, rather than being a problem, the scar tissue held the severed tendon in place and made the surgery much easier. In my post-surgery, heavily drugged with a painkiller state of mind I thought, "Now that will preach." Going through struggles together as a community creates the scar tissue of life. That scar tissue of life becomes like glue holding our broken and severed relationships in place so that healing can occur. That scar tissue of life fashions our unity and makes us better together. We are better together when we go through troubles together.

Third, we are better together when we each invite God to wipe away every tear from our eyes. The Patmos prophet declared that "God will wipe away every tear from their eyes" (7:17; see also Isaiah 25:8). In this heavenly vision, everyone is healed from all pain and hurt. Then, they are promised that they will never again experience any kind of suffering. Obviously, only in heaven can such a promise by God be kept. Pain and suffering are universal on this earth. But part of that vision can be true in this realm. We are better together when we each invite God to wipe away every tear from our eyes. We are better together when we invite God to transform faith communities and activist circles that have become places of pain into places of healing. Our communities must be spaces for healing. Healing comes from God. We must invite God to wipe the tears from our eyes.

We are better together . . .

Notes

1. Richard Smallwood, William Gaither, and Gloria Gaither, "Center of My Joy," 1997.

2. Leslie Scanlon, "Reconciliation and Justice: Allan Boesak Tells NEXT Conference Not to Be Afraid to Speak Truth," *The Presbyterian Outlook*, February 22, 2016, www.pres-outlook.org/2016/02/reconciliation-and-justice-allan-boesak-speaks-to-next-conferencegoers.

3. Richard A. Horsley, *Jesus and Empire: The Kingdom of God and the New World Disorder* (Minneapolis: Fortress, 2003), 28–29.

The Call to Mystic Moments
Resting in the Womb of God

That same day Jesus went out of the house and sat beside the sea. (Matthew 13:1)

Many years ago, I made my first visit to Waimanalo Beach on Oahu in the Hawaiian Islands.[1] This beach, nestled in a Native Hawaiian community, is set in a three-dimensional frame with mountains on one side and ocean on the other, blue sky above and sand below. I arrived exhausted from ministry and activism. The majestic natural beauty ministered to me in deep and mysterious ways. Feeling the heat of the bright and welcoming sun stimulated and enlivened my body. Walking in the cool and embracing sand focused and reinvigorated my mind. Listening to the soothing sound of the waves nurtured and rejuvenated my tired soul. The restorative power was exhilarating. This sense of mystical tranquility was intense while walking along the enchantingly beautiful Waimanalo Beach on Oahu. This beach is affectionately called "the healing beach" by friends who live on the island.[2]

I felt extremely secure and unconditionally loved. I felt like I could reach out and almost hold hands with God. While the waves caressed my weary spirit, the stresses of life were released, and I relished a profoundly refreshing sense of restfulness. I delighted in the awareness that I belonged. My weary soul had been embraced and caressed by the Creator through a spiritually embryonic homecoming experience.

I wanted to stay forever. Upon returning to the mainland, I could only say that I had been resting in the womb of God.

The ocean is the place in nature where I find the greatest spiritual rest and refreshment. In addition to the Pacific Ocean, I have basked in the soothing winds and calming sands of the Indian Ocean, Gulf of Mexico, Atlantic Ocean, and Mediterranean Sea, as well as the ocean-like quality of Lake Michigan and its sand dunes. I live in Minnesota, so the oceans are quite some distance. Most of us cannot travel to Hawaii or an ocean whenever we need a spiritual rejuvenation. And even in "paradise," there are problems and anxiety. Sometimes urgency precludes waiting until a scheduled retreat or a vacation to address the heaviness of life. We must seek therapy for our souls that can be experienced right where we live.

Jesus faced a similar dilemma. His hectic life left little room for ocean retreats. Even when he did try to get away, he would be interrupted. Jesus traveled to the Mediterranean coastal city of Tyre in Lebanon for some rest, and a woman in need of healing for her daughter barged into the home where he was staying and disrupted his attempt to find solitude (Mark 7:24-30). Yet, Jesus' life exemplified a way of finding contemplative spaces amid noisy and cluttered realities. In the first verse of Matthew 13, we see Jesus as he sat by the sea. By the second verse, he was surrounded by crowds. While Jesus was often by bodies of water seeking some solace, he would also hike into the mountains and hills. Sometimes, he would pray early in the morning. The crowds were the reality of Jesus' ministry work. Yet, he could find contemplative spaces to rest in the womb of God right where his life was occurring. Howard Thurman wrote of the importance of this:

> There must be always remaining in every[one's] life some
> place for the singing of angels—some place for that which

in itself is breathlessly beautiful and by an inherent prerogative, throwing all the rest of life into a new a creative relatedness—something that gathers up in itself all the freshets of experience from drab and commonplace areas of living and glows in one bright white light of penetrating beauty and meaning—then passes. The commonplace is shot through with new glory—old burdens become lighter, deep and ancient wounds lose much of the old, old hurting. A crown is placed over our heads that for the rest of our lives we are trying to grow tall enough to wear. Despite all the crassness of life, despite all the hardness of life, despite all of the harsh discords of life, life is saved by the singing of angels.[3]

I recommend mapping out contemplative spaces in daily life. I know where the lakes and walking paths are in Minneapolis so I can grab a quick hour or fifteen minutes of peace. I have learned how to shut my office door, even for a few minutes, to transport my mind and thoughts to a quieter zone. Our need for spiritual retreats, vacations, and regular meditation will not depart. Yet, sometimes the challenges of daily life or committed activism make these seem like luxuries at the time. So, we must also practice the discipline of finding, mapping, and using contemplative spaces nearby so we can hear the singing of angels and experience the rest found in the womb of God.

Racial justice action and beloved community need a foundation of contemplation and spirituality. Faith-inspired activists depend on a sense of the mystic to address the genuine experience of facing risks from being awake to injustice. Section 3 shares wisdom from the last moments in the lives of Jesus of Nazareth and Paul of Tarsus so we can navigate the intersection of the activist and mystic.

Notes

1. This section introduction has been adapted from Curtiss Paul DeYoung, "Ministered to . . . ," *Thin Places* 2, no. 101 (December 2019/January–February 2020), 1–2, ecumenical newsletter of Westminster Presbyterian Church, Minneapolis.

2. My friends in Hawai'i are Al and Kathy Miles.

3. Howard Thurman, *Meditations for Apostles of Sensitiveness* (Mills College, CA: Eucalyptus Press, 1948), 1.

CHAPTER 11

God's Time Zone

From noon on, darkness came over the whole land until three in the afternoon. And about three o'clock Jesus cried with a loud voice, "Eli, Eli, lema sabachthani?" that is, "My God, my God, why have you forsaken me?" . . . Then Jesus cried again with a loud voice and breathed his last. At that moment the curtain of the temple was torn in two, from top to bottom. The earth shook, and the rocks were split. The tombs also were opened, and many bodies of the saints who had fallen asleep were raised. After his resurrection they came out of the tombs and entered the holy city and appeared to many. (Matthew 27:45-46, 50-53)

Our lives are part of a greater narrative. Some things we can know only by reflecting after the event or encounter. There are ways that God is acting that we do not see in the present moment. Becoming aware that a divine story is also being written helps us to trust God. This text suggests that God operates in a divine time zone. Sometimes, history occurs in ways that are hard to understand. In 1994, a genocide occurred in Rwanda. Yet, later that same year, a nearly miraculous reconciliation moment occurred with the election of Nelson Mandela as president of South Africa. In God's time zone, surprising moments of reconciliation and justice can occur simultaneously with acts of inhumane injustices. This text is

THE RISK OF BEING WOKE

found in the midst of Matthew's recounting of a four-act drama about how God operates in time.

Act One: Time Progressed from Gethsemane to Golgotha

The first act in the drama began in the Garden of Gethsemane (Matthew 26:36-56) and finished on the cross at Golgotha (27:33). Less than twenty-four hours prior to his cry out to God in our text, Jesus was agitated, anxious, and experiencing severe grief. He took three of his disciples with him into the Garden of Gethsemane. As they entered Gethsemane, Jesus said, "My soul is deeply grieved, even to death; remain here, and stay awake with me" (26:38). Three times Jesus prayed to God pleading and agonizing for the cup of his death to be taken away. Three times Jesus submitted to the will of God. The march toward death had begun. God's time is not our time.

While the time from Gethsemane to Golgotha was short—less than twenty-four hours—it must have seemed long. Jesus' feeling of forsakenness and abandonment began in the Garden of Gethsemane and intensified as time progressed to Golgotha. In Jesus' moment of agonizing prayer in Gethsemane, his disciples slept. They emotionally and spiritually abandoned their friend Jesus. Finally, Jesus said to them, "The hour is at hand" (26:45). Time was marching toward death.

One of Jesus' trusted disciples arrived at the entrance to the garden and greeted Jesus with a kiss—a kiss of betrayal. Judas forsook Jesus by corrupting a symbol of intimate friendship as he identified Jesus to the ruling council's police force. Jesus was arrested and put on trial before the religious authorities. His closest friend watched from the shadows. But when asked about Jesus, Peter denied three times even knowing Jesus, and he abandoned his friend. Time was marching toward death.

Early in the morning, Jesus was found guilty, condemned to death, and handed over to the Roman Empire for execution. The legal system failed Jesus. The betrayer witnessed this act. Judas could not face his actions and took his own life. Judas forsook Jesus and his own future. In a final act of forsakenness, Governor Pilate, the representative of Caesar, washed his hands as a symbol of the Roman Empire's abandonment of any responsibility for what was soon to occur. Time was marching toward death.

For three hours, from noon until 3 p.m., the sky became like night. Jesus felt abandoned and forsaken by God. It was as though God turned away from a helpless Jesus. For the first time, Jesus experienced the sour taste of hopelessness in this moment of abandonment. Jesus saw the back of God rather than the face of the divine. While rejection by followers, friends, and family was likely not a surprise to Jesus, abandonment by God was a shock!

Jesus had eternally been in an intimate relationship with God. His conception was an act of godly interaction (1:18). At his baptism, God's voice declared, "This is my Son, the Beloved; with whom I am well pleased" (3:17). Again, at the transfiguration, "This is my Son, the Beloved" (17:5). Just the night before in the Garden of Gethsemane, Jesus had one of his most intense moments and intimate encounters with God. In less than twenty-four hours, Jesus went from intimacy to isolation, from faithfulness to forsakenness, from a unique and amazing relationship with God to utter abandonment. While Jesus knew his death was near, I do not think he could have predicted the feeling of abandonment. I do not think he could have dreamed or imagined, anticipated, conceived of, expected, or envisioned such a moment on the road less traveled.

Jesus reached into his memory to the Hebrew prayer book for words to express this new, strange, and troubling experience. In the Gospel of Matthew, Jesus recited the opening lines of Psalm 22 using a mixture of the more formal biblical Hebrew and the vernacular of Aramaic. Rather than simply reciting this prayer of King

David in the liturgical language of Hebrew, Jesus translated the eloquence of the language of the temple to the earthiness of his own daily expression in Aramaic. "My God, my God, why have you forsaken me?" (27:46).[1] The language of worship could not express the torturous reality that Jesus was experiencing. Only the street vernacular, the dialect of the depths of his soul, could be used to communicate the inner pain and tragedy that was now consuming him. Jesus cried out from Psalm 22.

Since I am not conversant in French or Creole, I was dependent on a translator when I visited the French Caribbean island of Guadeloupe. One Sunday, we attended a church service. Given my linguistic curiosity, I asked my translator to tell me when people spoke French and when they spoke Creole. A woman in the congregation prayed out loud with much fervor. My translator shared with me that the prayer began in French and ended in Creole. I asked why two languages were used in prayer. I was informed that French was used to speak of the majesty of God. But Creole was used when speaking more personally of suffering and struggles. Creole was the language of the heart. The Guadeloupian woman and Jesus both moved from the language of worship to the vernacular of the depths of their souls when praying about the most personal and painful of situations.[2]

Time was marching toward death. In Gethsemane, the disciples did not know that Jesus' death was a day away. Plans were already in motion for a betrayal by Judas and the arrest by soldiers, which would lead to the death of Jesus of Nazareth. This would dramatically alter their lives. We do not always know what may already be in motion. I had an experience of not knowing what was already in motion when I began my work as the CEO of the Minnesota Council of Churches. I was just three weeks into my new job on August 4, 2017, when my wife, Karen, and I celebrated our wedding anniversary. I did not know that, while we were celebrating, three members of an Illinois-based white supremacist terrorist militia group called The White Rabbits were already on their way to Minnesota with plans to bomb the Dar al Farooq Mosque in Bloomington, Minnesota. The lives of Minnesota Muslims would be traumatized, leading to months of uncertainty and fear. The trajectory of my leadership at the council would be dramatically altered. We do not know what is waiting for us in life. But in the twenty-four hours prior to crucifixion, Jesus knew.

As time progressed from Gethsemane to Golgotha, Jesus was rejected and condemned in countless additional ways. In less than twenty-four hours, Jesus found himself stripped of everything that defines our understanding of human life: relationships, dignity, and decency. The culmination of this short but shameful, brief yet broken journey from Gethsemane to Golgotha was Jesus being nailed to a cross—the ultimate act of human rejection, degradation, and forsakenness. Jesus had been crushed and crucified by the empire.

Act Two: Time Paused from Noon until Three

"From noon on, darkness came over the whole land until three in the afternoon" (27:45). Time stood still. The lights turned off. Everything stopped. All the various normal activities that took place on planet Earth were put on hold. God pressed the PAUSE button on the heavenly time machine. Time paused so that all those in heaven and on earth could focus all their attention on the central act of all time—Jesus was dying on a cross. At the very last moment, Jesus uttered, "My God," which signaled that he was praying.

When tragedy occurs, life pauses. In moments of crisis, all our attention is required. Everything else is put on hold. The morning of August 5, 2017, I was informed of the bombing at the nearby mosque in Bloomington. I was summoned to an interfaith religious leaders' press conference. When I arrived, I learned that Imam Mohamed Omar's office had been bombed as morning prayers were scheduled to begin. Thank God no one died. But the imam and the members of the mosque were devastated as they experienced the effects of the militia's intended terror. The entire community was on pause as the police and the FBI were on site and mosque leaders and other clergy were speaking to the media.

Jesus cried out a second time at about 3 p.m. "Then Jesus cried out with a loud voice and breathed his last" (27:50). After his prayer to God and his death, the darkness ended and light returned. The pause ended, and God resumed the flow of time.

Act Three: Time Moves Both Forward and Backward

When the divine pause ended, a strange cosmic moment occurred. "At that moment the curtain of the temple was torn in two, from top to bottom. The earth shook, and the rocks were split. The tombs also were opened, and many bodies of the saints who had fallen asleep were raised. After his resurrection they came out of the tombs and entered the holy city and appeared to many" (27:51-53).

Time moved forward so that normal life resumed. Simultaneously, time began to move backward, undoing certain historic realities. The curtain of the temple was torn in half from the top to bottom, undoing the historic reality that blocked women, people of other cultures, and those considered outcasts from having full access to holy places (Ephesians 2:14-15). Graves broke open, and people who had died and been buried felt their hearts start to beat again. Empty and dry veins felt blood flowing again. Collapsed lungs started to feel air pump them up again. Women and men who had long been dead stood up again and praised God again. As time moved backward, God was undoing the historic reality of their deaths. God reversed death and returned life. Time also moved forward as the Roman execution squad declared their faith at the sight of these cosmic events: "Truly this man was God's Son!" (27:54).

In our Western understanding of time, death is the end. In God's time zone, death is not final. In God's time zone, the crucifixion was not death, but rather it was birth. New life, new possibilities, and new hopes were born as a result of the cross. Things thought forever gone can be restored in God's time zone. God can witness life in the midst of death. The resurrections of those long dead were a signal that God was at work.

On that August day at Dar al Farooq Mosque, I said to the media that "an attack on a mosque is an attack on a synagogue, it's an attack on a church, it's an attack on all faith communities."[3] Time moved forward as the mosque developed new networks of support in its neighborhood (including several churches) and became a leader in the Twin Cities for interfaith community organizing. My leadership role at the Minnesota Council of Churches quickly became more centrally focused on interfaith efforts. The perpetrators of the crime were apprehended and convicted in federal court.

Time also moved backward as two of the three racist perpetrators became repentant, pled guilty, helped the prosecution, and fully accepted the consequences of their actions. They disavowed their white supremacist beliefs and hateful actions. This caused mosque leaders to temper their calls for justice with a request for clemency. In what was said by the judge and attorneys to be a rare act in a federal courtroom, Imams Mohamed Omar and Asad Zaman were joined by Rabbi Adam Spilker and me at the sentencing to make witness statements that requested less time in prison and offered expressions of forgiveness and grace to the assailants.[4] Any past history of religious rivalry was reversed, leading to our act of Abrahamic unity.

When we face our Gethsemane moments, when we feel like time has passed and we are all alone and forsaken, we can call to our God, even if we are questioning if God is there. God will hear our cry. In God's time zone, our dead ends are not final; our sin is not final; our mess is not final; and the power of the empire is not final. In God's time zone, time can be reversed. In those places where we feel hopeless, like we have died . . . we can stand up again. We can shout again. We can sing songs again. We can praise God again.

Act Four: The Window of Easter

I struggle with the apparent abandonment of Jesus by God in this text. African Methodist Episcopal Church episcopal supervisor Jessica Kendall Ingram notes, "At the end of his journey, hanging on an old rugged cross, when Jesus asked the question, 'My God, my God, why have you forsaken me?' God did not bother to answer. There was silence on Calvary."[5] She makes it so plain; God did not bother to answer. I am troubled by God's apparent absence.

There must be another message behind this word of forsakenness that can be seen only by peering through the window of Easter. Even a quick glance through the window of Easter reveals that God was not absent. While Jesus could not have expected or predicted his feeling of forsakenness . . . God did not forsake him! God was silent, not absent. God's silence was not forsakenness. God's silence was not powerlessness. God's silence did not mean a lack of action.

When viewed through the window of Easter, we can see that God's silence had a purpose. God could have intervened. God could have rescued Jesus from the cross. But God restrained Godself. God showed great self-control for three hours as the earth went dark. How do I know that God restrained Godself? The moment that Jesus died—*boom*—God let loose: sunlight, torn curtain, earthquake, tombs broke open, dead saints lived, and the Roman execution squad expressed faith in Jesus. It is "the death of Jesus which triggers the resurrection of the saints" and the declaration of faith by the executioners.[6]

God might have been silent, but God was not absent. God showed great restraint because Jesus' death had great purpose.

That purpose was resurrection. Rescuing Jesus from the cross would have been a singular event. Resurrection was an eternal event. Without Jesus' death, there would be no resurrection. Resurrection declares that death does not have the final word. Resurrection from death by Caesar declared that oppressors did not have the final word. Resurrection declares that rejection is not the final word. We may feel forsaken by God, but silence does not mean absence. God is always on the scene. God is always with us. If God goes silent and feels absent, you better get ready because you may be on the verge of resurrection. In God's time zone, resurrection is the final act in life's drama. Howard Thurman wrote that faith "holds within its grasp the past and the future as a single moment in time."[7] Standing in God's time zone, we hold on to our timely and timeless faith in God (Eloi)! Amen.

Notes

1. In Mark 13:34, Jesus quotes Psalm 22 fully in Aramaic. Mark is considered likely the original form.

2. My translator in Guadeloupe was Marquise Armand.

3. "Minnesota Mosque Hit by Early-Morning Explosion," *New York Times*, August 5, 2017, www.nytimes.com/2017/08/05/us/minnesota-mosque-explo sion.html.

4. Andy Mannix, "After Pleas for Leniency, Mosque Bombers Receive 14, 16 Years," *StarTribune*, April 12, 2022, www.news.yahoo.com/pleas-leniency-mosque-bombers-receive-205300493.html.

5. Jessica Kendall Ingram, "How to Handle the Silence of God," *The African American Pulpit* 6, no. 2 (Spring 2003), 48.

6. Review by Raymond E. Brown of Donald Senior, *The Passion Narrative of Matthew*, in *Catholic Biblical Quarterly* 38 (1976), 328, quoted in Leon Morris, *The Gospel According to Matthew* (Grand Rapids, MI: Eerdmans, 1992), 725.

7. Howard Thurman, *The Inward Journey: Meditations on the Spiritual Quest* (New York: Harper & Brothers, 1961), 23.

CHAPTER 12

God's Preparation for a Future Yet Unseen

"It is finished." Then he bowed his head and gave up his spirit. (John 19:30)

Then Jesus, crying with a loud voice, said, "Father, into your hands I commend my spirit." Having said this, he breathed his last. (Luke 23:46)

These two Gospel writers described Jesus' final moments. In full control, Jesus determined his final moments on the cross and then peered into the darkness and saw eternity. Most often the future cannot be seen. One cannot know if an action for racial justice will achieve what is hoped for. I suggest an experience of eternity transforms our perceptions of reality and enables us to embrace future possibilities.

Jesus' words, "It is finished," bear a sense of finality. For the person who is dying, the finality of death can be experienced as a release or relief. Crucifixion was a very painful process of death. The severe suffering on the cross was now ending for Jesus, and there was a sense of relief and release when he said, "It is finished." Perhaps when Jesus said this phrase, it was a way to mark the end of a life. His life was now finished. There is a finality to death whether experienced as relief and release, shock and sadness, or remembrance and celebration. The word for "finish" used by John was used only in these verses. A more accurate definition would be that Jesus was saying that his life and ministry were completely done or fully accomplished. The apostle Paul captured the essence of this meaning in his own life when he wrote—echoing Jesus' words, "it is finished"—"I have fought the good fight; I have finished the race; I have kept the faith" (2 Timothy 4:7). Jesus had completed the work he came to do. Jesus stated with confidence that he had fully accomplished the purpose of his life. He was finished.

I have attempted to interpret and understand these final words of Jesus as recorded in the Gospel of John. Yet, I believe that Jesus himself interpreted his words from the cross. How he died interpreted what he said. When people died on a cross, they would stop breathing and their heads would involuntarily drop. Jesus reversed this. He bowed his head, and then he died. "He bowed his head and gave up his spirit" (19:30). Jesus was in full control of his body and spirit until the end, until he decided it was finished. He bowed his head in prayer and then voluntarily gave up his spirit. Death did not happen until Jesus signaled it was time.

A better translation is that "he handed over his spirit."[1] Jesus bowed in prayer and handed over his spirit to God. The chief priests handed Jesus over to Pilate for interrogation (John 18:30). Pilate handed Jesus over for crucifixion (19:16). In each use of this phrase, one is handed over so something else can happen. When Jesus said, "It is finished" and handed over his spirit to God, he was saying that his job on earth was done. He handed over his life to God, waiting for his next assignment. Jesus had said during his ministry, "The hour has come for the Son of Man to be glorified. Very truly, I tell you, unless a grain of wheat falls into the earth and dies, it remains just a single grain; but if it dies, it bears much fruit" (12:23-24). When Jesus said it was finished, he was saying that one phase (his earthly life) ended, so that the next phase could begin.

When Jesus bowed his head, perhaps it was a nod of acknowledgment, a gesture.[2] Perhaps it was a nod that declared life follows death. Perhaps it was a nod that said I must finish so that Pentecost can happen and the church can be born. Or maybe it was more personal. Maybe Jesus bowed his head in a nod to his mother, John, Mary Magdalene, and the other women gathered at the cross. With a nod of his head, Jesus said, I will see you in a few days. It was a nod toward resurrection. What is seen in the present is not the end. Jesus' nod was an acknowledgment of a future yet unseen.

In the Darkness, What Can Be Seen

In the Good Friday service of the Seven Last Words from the Cross, "it is finished" is word six. The final and seventh word is from Luke, "Father, into your hands I commend my spirit" (23:46). It was at noon that Friday when Jesus spoke his final words. From noon to 3 p.m., the sun stopped shining and darkness came over the land. The sky went dark at the brightest moment in the day. The sunlight disappeared. In what could be interpreted as a reference to this moment, the prophet Amos wrote, "On that day, says the Lord GOD, I will make the sun go down at noon and darken the earth in broad daylight" (8:9). In the darkness, Jesus saw eternity. Jesus prayed Psalm 31, which was used for evening prayers: "Into your hand I commit my spirit; you have redeemed me, O LORD, faithful God" (31:5). Jesus prayed from the cross as he had done the night before in the Garden of Gethsemane when he prayed to accept God's will (Luke 22:42-44).

As Jesus prayed, the temple curtain protecting the Holy of Holies began to tear. In the darkness, people in the temple courts heard the ripping sound of the curtain tearing. The Holy of the Holies was the place that represented the presence of God. It could be entered only by the high priest once a year on Yom Kippur, the day of atonement. In my imagination, in the darkness, I see the spirit of God bursting through the tear in the curtain, coming to Jesus with open hands. In the darkness, Jesus saw the God of eternity and cried out, "Into your hands I commend my spirit." The one who had been "betrayed into human hands" (Luke 9:44) now placed himself in the hands of God.[3]

In the darkness, the people at the cross saw a transformed reality. The Roman soldier and the gathered crowds saw Jesus in a new way. The Roman soldier, who had seen Jesus as a convicted felon, now saw a righteous man and proclaimed, "Certainly this man was innocent" (23:47). The crowd of spectators that was gathered to watch the crucifixion of Jesus as a tragic and sordid form of entertainment now saw his innocence and were horrified by their own fascination with Roman crucifixions. They repented and demonstrated remorse by beating their breasts (23:48). Biblical scholars Bruce Malina and Richard Rohrbaugh note, "Breast-beating was normally a gesture of women rather than men, apparently used by the latter only in the direst of circumstances."[4] When the crowd saw Jesus embrace eternity, circumstances became dire. They experienced the transformation of reality. They saw Jesus in the very intimate moment of transition and felt the palpable presence of God. The words exclaimed by Martin Luther King Jr. the night before he was killed somehow seem relevant here: "Only when it is dark enough, can you see the stars."[5] In the darkness, we experience a transformed reality and see possibility.

What If?

When I was contemplating the words of this Lukan text, I heard on the radio the song "What If" performed by Minneapolis musical artist Prince and his band 3rdEyeGirl.[6] Prince released the song in 2015, one year before his untimely death. It was a cover of a song written and originally performed by contemporary Christian artist Nichole Nordeman. Her song describes the tension between faith and doubt regarding the Jesus narrative. The song is a series of what-if questions. Prince transformed her pensive haunting song into an urgent intense cry that demands answers to the eternal quandary. What if Jesus' death was the end of the story? What if there was something beyond death? Prince stepped into the darkness vocally and with his wailing guitar and pleaded, "What if?"

At the cross, the crowds and the soldiers watched Jesus die in the darkness. What if this was all there was? What if the story of Jesus ended? What if there was something beyond death? The question—what if there was something more?—informed the remaining actions described in Luke 23. The Spirit of Jesus was held in the hands of God. If death was not the end, Jesus' spirit must be protected. The Roman soldier declared the innocence of Jesus, and the people of the city repented. If there was more story to be told, they would become followers. "All his acquaintances, including the women who had followed him from Galilee, stood at a distance watching these things" (23:49). If death was not the end, they were eyewitnesses to the death of Jesus. Joseph of Arimathea secured the body of Jesus. Typically, burial for capital punishment victims was denied by Roman authorities given the fear of creating a martyr. Bodies from crosses were thrown into common graves and sometimes eaten by birds. But Joseph gained permission. He personally took the body of Jesus off the cross and laid him in an empty tomb cut into the rock. If there was something beyond death, the body of Jesus was secure and discoverable.

Luke noted that "it was the day of Preparation" (23:54). Jewish people were preparing for Shabbat. Homes were being cleaned. Final work was being finished as the Passover Sabbath arrived. The women from Galilee were preparing spices and ointments to apply to the body of Jesus after the Sabbath. Strangely, it was as though the seen—the hectic day of Preparation activities—was preparing for the unseen. Holy Saturday became a time of waiting, an in-between time, between what was and what might be. What if this was all there was? Jesus was dead, buried, and gone. What if there was something beyond this moment?

Racial justice activists face the what-ifs of life's journey. What if our protests lead to no change? What if our legislative proposals are blocked or compromised? What if the media move on to the next story? What if the attention span of the populace is too short? What if injustice re-entrenches and reoccurs? What if little change or no change is all there is?

At such moments—and they will come, often—we need to peer into the metaphorical darkness. We need to put on the lens of eternity. We need to see a vision of a transformed reality. We need to embrace the day of preparation for a racially just future yet unseen. There must be something more! There must be hope!

Notes

1. Gail R. O'Day, "The Gospel of John," in *The New Interpreter's Bible* vol. 9, ed. Leander E. Keck (Nashville: Abingdon, 1995), 833.

2. J. Ramsey Michaels, *The Gospel of John* (Grand Rapids, MI: Eerdmans, 2010), 964.

3. R. Alan Culpepper, "The Gospel of Luke," in *The New Interpreter's Bible* vol. 9, ed. Leander E. Keck (Nashville: Abingdon, 1995), 461.

4. Bruce J. Malina and Richard L. Rohrbaugh, *Social-Science Commentary on the Synoptic Gospels* (Minneapolis: Fortress, 1992), 409.

5. Martin Luther King Jr., "I See the Promised Land," in *A Testament of Hope: The Essential Writings and Speeches of Martin Luther King Jr.*, ed. James M. Washington (San Francisco: HarperSanFrancisco, 1986), 280.

6. Prince and 3rdEyeGirl, "What If?", www.youtube.com/watch?v=CPqkBVxNQ_k.

CHAPTER 13

When the Empire Strikes Back

As for me, I am already being poured out as a libation, and the time of my departure has come. I have fought the good fight; I have finished the race; I have kept the faith. From now on there is reserved for me the crown of righteousness, which the Lord, the righteous judge, will give to me on that day, and not only to me but also to all who have longed for his appearing.

Do your best to come to me soon, for Demas, in love with this present world, has deserted me and gone to Thessalonica; Crescens has gone to Galatia, Titus to Dalmatia. Only Luke is with me. Get Mark and bring him with you, for he is useful in my ministry. I have sent Tychicus to Ephesus. When you come, bring the cloak that I left with Carpus at Troas, also the books, and above all the parchments. Alexander the coppersmith did me great harm; the Lord will pay him back for his deeds. You also must beware of him, for he strongly opposed our message.

At my first defense no one came to my support, but all deserted me. May it not be counted against them! But the Lord stood by me and gave me strength, so that through me the message might be fully proclaimed and all the gentiles might hear it. So I was rescued from the lion's mouth. The Lord will rescue me from every evil attack and save me for his heavenly kingdom. To him be the glory forever and ever. Amen. . . . Do your best to come before winter. (2 Timothy 4:6-18, 21)

Scholars debate whether 2 Timothy was penned by the apostle Paul or by someone writing under the name of Paul. Yet, among those who question the Pauline authorship of the letter are many who would say that the intensely personal nature of our text leads them to believe that this is at the least an authentic fragment from the hand of the apostle. Another point of discussion concerns whether this text is Paul writing while under house arrest in Rome as described at the end of the Acts of the Apostles. Or is this a later imprisonment under much harsher conditions, just prior to his execution? According to tradition, this happened when Nero was emperor. I am approaching the text as though these words were written by Paul while imprisoned under much more brutal realities than house arrest just prior to his death.

The Context

To fully understand and appreciate our text, it is important to consider the context in which it was written. The context in which we find Paul in a Roman prison was the military presence and political domination of the Roman Empire. These daily realities shaped the apostle Paul's entire life. The Roman Empire ruled as though it was divinely ordained to civilize the world. Jews were among those ruled by Rome. Jews were regarded by the Roman elite as people born to be slaves. Jews faced extreme bias and experienced the brutally abusive oppression of Rome.[1]

The apostle Paul was a colonial subject of Rome. In Acts, Paul was quoted saying he was a citizen of Rome (22:25). Even though Roman citizenship offered some benefits for a colonized subject, Paul still experienced daily life as an oppressed Jew. (African American citizens of the United States still face racial discrimination.) In his own writings, Paul never claimed Roman citizenship. Paul's ethnic and religious identity was rooted in his Jewishness— "circumcised on the eighth day, a member of the people of Israel, of the tribe of Benjamin, a Hebrew born of Hebrews; as to the law, a Pharisee" (Philippians 3:5). This Jewish identity assured his colonized and oppressed status, and he likely felt terrorized at times by the Roman government.

One day on the road to Damascus, Paul's experience of colonization was interrupted by a life-changing encounter with a resurrected Jesus, the crucified one, now alive (Acts 9:3-16). Crucifixion was a brutal symbol of Roman rule. Jesus was crucified as a revolutionary leading an uprising against Roman domination. Like our history of lynching in the United States, crucifixion was designed to intimidate and terrorize a subject people. The crucifixion of Jesus was meant to have the same effect. As Paul wrote in Galatians 3:1, "It was before your eyes that Jesus Christ was publicly exhibited as crucified!"

On that road to Damascus, Paul encountered Jesus, whose Roman state-sponsored crucifixion had been reversed by a more powerful and completely just God. The empire did not have the final word! This logic fueled Paul's preaching. Death by Rome was reversed through resurrection by God. Therefore, the death of one's identity could be revived and returned through Christ to its original design as a human identity created in the image of God. The resurrection meant that one's empire identity could be switched to an identity in Jesus Christ. Paul wrote, "We regard no one from a human point of view"; that is, we regard no one from a dominant, empire point of view (2 Corinthians 5:16). Therefore, Paul preached that reconciliation transformed colonized persons through healing their identity and replacing a forced colonial loyalty with faith in Jesus Christ.

Paul and the early followers of a crucified and resurrected Jesus went into oppressed Jewish communities throughout the Roman Empire preaching the healing word of reconciliation. They established embryonic congregations as laboratories of healing for oppressed Jews to decolonize and recover from the harmful effects of colonialism. This was particularly important where oppression had been internalized. After embracing a process of their own individual and communal healing as Jews, these early Jewish followers of Jesus reached out to Romans who were members of the oppressing group and Greeks who were beneficiaries of the empire. The apostle Paul and first-century Jewish Christians believed that, through the death on a cross and the resurrection of Jesus, even a colonizing Roman with power and privilege could be transformed by God's reconciling grace.

As Romans and Greeks embraced their own decolonizing process, they replaced their loyalty to the empire with loyalty to Jesus Christ. Caesar could no longer be their savior. They rejected the privileges that go with power and position and joined with those who were colonized. Romans and Greeks stepped into the homes of Jews as guests and as equals. Their privileged perspectives and powerful positions were dispensed with and exchanged for the bonds of family. Empire privileges had no place in the church. Biblical scholar Richard Horsley notes that the first-century church was forming "more egalitarian social relations that cut across the fundamental social hierarchies of the imperial order, between Greeks and barbarians (including Jews), between free and slaves, and between male and female. . . . Paul was, in effect, building an international anti-imperial movement of an alternative society based in local communities."[2]

Precisely at such moments, when societal transformation seems just around the corner, is when the empire strikes back.

The civil rights movement had several such moments. In 1963, there was a successful direct action campaign in Birmingham, Alabama, and then Dr. Martin Luther King Jr.'s "I Have a Dream" speech, which made an integrated and reconciled beloved community seem on the verge of breaking forth into US history. The empire struck back in the killing of four little girls attending Sunday school in the basement of the Sixteenth Street Baptist Church in Birmingham.

In 1965, Malcolm X visited the voter registration drive in Selma, Alabama, signaling his willingness to work with the civil rights movement and Martin Luther King in what could have become a powerful alliance for racial justice and reconciliation. The empire struck back in the assassination of El Hajj Malik El Shabazz (Malcolm X).

In 1968, multiracial anti-poverty movements emerged in a united effort to address injustice and radically transform the economic and racial realities of the United States. The empire struck back in the assassinations of Martin Luther King Jr. and Robert Kennedy.

At times like this is when the empire strikes back. On the verge of success is when the empire strikes back. At the daybreak of a new era is when the empire strikes back. The moment in which Caesar feels vulnerable is when the empire strikes back. I suggest that the success of the first-century church created such powerful conditions for social change that the empire had to strike back. And the empire did strike back at the first-century church. If tradition is correct, in the early 60s, the apostles Peter, James the brother of Jesus, and Paul were all killed by the Roman Empire or the empire's proxies.[3]

The Text

If we are to demand radical reconciliation—that is, a reconciliation that addresses the roots of racial injustice; a reconciliation that reverses the categories of powerful and powerless, colonizer and colonized; a reconciliation that questions the foundations of our modern empires—then we need to prepare for the moment when the empire strikes back. Our text helps us understand what happens to advocates of racial justice when the empire strikes back and how we must be prepared to respond. Second Timothy 4 was written by Paul after the Roman Empire imprisoned him and put him on trial. Paul was experiencing what happens when the empire strikes back. These are likely the final words written by the apostle Paul. They are directed to Timothy—his closest companion in ministry. But more than that, Timothy had become a son to Paul. This correspondence has the feel of a letter between parent and child. Paul addressed the letter "To Timothy, my beloved child" (2 Timothy 1:2; see also 1 Corinthians 4:17).

Paul believed his death would occur in the near future—"the time of my departure has come" (2 Timothy 4:6). Perhaps he had already received a death sentence from Rome. He asked Timothy to come quickly . . . to "come before winter" (4:21). We can hear the urgency in his words. Why before winter? The change of seasons affected one's ability to travel. There was no travel on the Adriatic or Mediterranean seas from November to March. There were too many storms. Even September to October and April to May could be risky. There was a small window of opportunity for travel by sea. Travel often took several months. One had to plan accordingly if needing to go by ship. Paul sent this letter to Timothy knowing that by the time he received it he would be required to expedite his travel to Rome.

Paul wanted Timothy by his side in his final days. These would be their last moments together. Typically, sons buried their fathers. Paul wanted his beloved son with him to make the final arrangements. If Timothy were to delay his travel, he might not be able to make it to Rome until spring. His beloved mentor and father in the ministry would likely already be dead.

I discovered this text through my mentor, preaching professor James Earl Massey, who for many years preached each fall from the verse, "Come before winter." In his sermon he noted, "This verse brings a certain truth into sharp focus: it tells us that there is a time of opportunity to do some things in life; it tells us that the time for doing some things is a passing time; it etches sharply the need for the immediate with regard to some things. . . . It tells us that the winter of reality closes in at a certain season, that things left hanging and undone, when that season changes must remain hanging and undone. Opportunity is a passing reality."[4]

Paul's urgent cry to Timothy to come before winter was not only about the literal season of winter. It was not only about the wintertime of his life as he faced death. I believe that Paul was also facing the possibility that this could be the winter, the death, of the church's ministry of reconciliation in the Roman Empire. When the empire strikes back, we are knocked down. The summertime of success soon becomes the wintertime of setback. Paul was on trial and held in prison. It is possible that he had been beaten and tortured. He knew his life and ministry were nearly done. Was he also giving up hope for the ministry of reconciliation in the empire?

What happens to us when the empire strikes back?

People desert us. Biblical scholar Luke Timothy Johnson writes, "Far from emboldening his coworkers, his imprisonment now seems to make them flee and abandon him out of shame or cowardice."[5] Paul cried out, "Demas . . . has deserted me . . . Only Luke is with me" (4:10, 11). Demas was the sixth person identified as deserting Paul in the letters to Timothy (1 Timothy 1:20; 2 Timothy 1:15, 2:17). Speaking of his trial, Paul exclaimed, "No one came to my support, but all deserted me" (4:16). In a culture where it was customary to have your friends with you in the courtroom, Paul stood trial all alone.

What happens to us when the empire strikes back?

We feel depressed.

Paul had waxed eloquent: "I have fought the good fight; I have finished the race; I have kept the faith" (4:7). His words are beautiful and poetic. It was the climax of his message . . . the final flourish . . . the hoop! But then the tone and the feel of Paul's words make a dramatic shift. In fact, beginning in verse 9, what we read hardly sounds like Scripture. Nowhere else in the New Testament do we read such raw requests and recollections. Paul's words were blunt, raw, lacking nuance, unedited, unpolished, unrefined, and even undignified. His voice was honest, transparent, vulnerable, and without filters. Paul was feeling the despair of desertion and betrayal by close friends. He was lonely and depressed living in the conditions of a dark and damp prison cell.

I can imagine that it was Luke writing as Paul dictated. When Paul finished his final flourish (4:8), he took the letter from Luke as though he was finished. Then, in his own handwriting, he quickly and carelessly added these emotion-filled, personal, and painful final remarks. Perhaps only with his son, Timothy, could he be so unfiltered and transparent.

The departure of Demas, who was a member of Paul's inner circle, was particularly devastating. The word Paul used for Demas's desertion was the same word that Jesus borrowed from Psalm 22 when he was on the cross and spoke of his forsakenness. Paul used this same word again when noting that he was deserted and all alone at his trial. Paul felt so forsaken, betrayed, alone, and depressed that he used the language of Jesus from the cross, "My God, my God, why have you forsaken me?" (Mark 15:34). Some may refuse to consider the possibility that Paul could be depressed. I disagree. Paul was human. When the empire strikes back, we experience real human feelings.

In our text, Paul makes three specific requests of Timothy: to bring his cloak, his scrolls and parchments, and his coworker Mark. I see these as answers to the question: What must we do when the empire strikes back?

What must we do when the empire strikes back?

We must take care of our physical health.

Paul asked Timothy to bring him his cloak. This coat would have been like a blanket with a hole in it for one's head. It was used when it rained, or it was cold. Paul must have left his cloak in Troas when it was warm. Now, he was sitting in a cold, damp prison with winter soon arriving. He needed his cloak for warmth. Paul knew that to deal with the stressful season he was in, he must take care of his physical needs. He needed his cloak for warmth. When we are filled with anxiety, we must care for our health and physical well-being. Regular exercise and healthy food are essential.

What must we do when the empire strikes back? We must attend to our mental and spiritual needs.

Paul's first request reminds us of the importance of caring for our daily physical needs when going through difficult times. His second request was for his books and parchments. Books refer to scrolls. The same word was used for the scrolls of the Hebrew Scriptures. Parchments were a collection of papyrus sheets in book form. They were much sturdier than scrolls and were made popular by Christians as they were used for various books of the New Testament. We do not know which books and parchments Paul asked for. Perhaps they were books of the day. Likely they were Scriptures, sayings of Jesus, early versions of the Gospels, or even some of Paul's own writings bound as parchments. Paul knew that to face the challenges of a trial before the Supreme Court of the Roman Empire, his mind must be sharp. He needed the discipline of study, particularly of the Scriptures. He must be able to think critically in the courtroom and be assured of God's word on the matter. In times of stress, we need to keep our minds fresh and focused so that we can think critically and pray more intensely and intentionally.

What must we do when the empire strikes back? We need to surround ourselves with healthy relationships.

The third request Paul made was for Timothy to bring Mark with him. Mark was the son of Mary of Jerusalem and a cousin of Barnabas. Some believe that Paul asked for Mark to replace his own teaching and pastoral presence in Rome after his death. But I see something else, as well. With Demas and others deserting him, Paul was feeling relational stress. Mark represented a reconciled and healthy relationship. Paul and Barnabas, the two apostles of reconciliation, split up their partnership because of a disagreement over Mark's value to their team. Barnabas wanted to continue with his cousin while Paul did not find him dependable. The author of Acts wrote, "The disagreement became so sharp that they parted company" (15:39). Yet, it seems that later Paul and Barnabas reconciled, and Paul came to greatly value Mark (Colossians 4:10). So, Mark represents reconciled and healthy relationships. Paul knew that, if he was going to stay strong, he would need to be surrounded by healthy relationships.

The call for Timothy and Mark to come meant that Paul also knew the work of reconciliation was bigger and broader than just him. When the empire strikes back . . . the empire wants us to believe that it is all about us. That if we are stopped, the ministry of reconciliation is finished. It was not wintertime for reconciliation. Rather it was time for a "generational transition."[6] Reconciliation was not finished. Paul and other leaders had been mentoring Jews, Greeks, and Romans, both women and men. This next generation would pick up the work. It was time for Paul to pass it on.

The Subtext

Our text sits amid a broader context where a powerful and radical reconciliation movement was growing in the Roman Empire. Our text is a clear example that it is at just such a moment when the empire strikes back. So, we need to be prepared physically, mentally, spiritually, and relationally. We have examined our text in its context. But a subtext—an underlying theme in a piece of writing—is also buried within this text.

This subtext answers a final question: What does God do when the empire strikes back?

Paul wrote, "But the Lord stood by me and gave me strength" (2 Timothy 4:17). Paul used very personal language implying that he felt the divine physical mystical presence of Jesus by his side.

Demas and others may have abandoned Paul, but Jesus always accompanied him. The crucified one, now resurrected, was standing at Paul's side. The empire did not have the final word!

Paul facing death in a Roman prison does not represent the first time the empire struck back. The crucifixion of Jesus itself was evidence of what the empire was willing to do to keep its power and dominance. When the empire struck back . . . Jesus found himself dead on a cross. Yet, a more powerful God raised Jesus up from the dead and through his resurrection reminds us that the empire never has the final word! So as the risen Lord stood at Paul's side, he was reminding the apostle that he could deliver him from the lion's mouth—that is, Caesar and the empire.[7] He gave Paul the strength and dynamic energy to witness God's reconciliation in the Supreme Court of the Roman Empire.

Conclusion

We do not know if Timothy made it to Rome before winter. I am sure he made every effort. Perhaps, the three requests Paul made and the reminder of God's presence were more for Timothy than they were for Paul himself. Paul was in his final season of life, while Timothy had many seasons yet ahead. Paul wanted Timothy to be prepared for the journey as an advocate of social justice and reconciliation.

This word is also for us. If we embrace the call to racial justice and radical reconciliation, there will be moments when the empire strikes back. In those seasons, in those winters of discouragement and struggle, let us commit ourselves to Paul's practical words to be healthy people in our bodies, minds, spirits, and relationships. And then, with that commitment, we can count on the fact that Jesus is always standing beside us.

The good news is that after winter comes spring! Seasons change.

Notes

1. An expanded description of the first-century context of the Roman Empire can be found in Allan Aubrey Boesak and Curtiss Paul DeYoung, *Radical Reconciliation: Beyond Political Pietism and Christian Quietism* (Maryknoll, NY: Orbis Books, 2012), 12–23, 79–85.

2. Richard A. Horsley, *Jesus and Empire: The Kingdom of God and the New World Disorder* (Minneapolis: Fortress, 2003), 133.

3. For the deaths of Peter and Paul see John Dominic Crossan and Jonathan L. Reed, *In Search of Paul: How Jesus's Apostle Opposed Rome's Empire with God's Kingdom* (San Francisco: HarperSanFrancisco, 2004), 400–402.

4. James Earl Massey, *Views from the Mountain: Select Writings of James Earl Massey*, ed. Barry L. Callen and Curtiss Paul DeYoung (Glendora, CA: Aldersgate Press, 2018), 82.

5. Luke Timothy Johnson, *The First and Second Letter to Timothy*, Anchor Yale Bible 35A (New Haven, CT: Yale University Press, 2001, 2008), 450.

6. Ibid.

7. William D. Mounce, *Pastoral Epistles*, Word Biblical Commentary 46 (Grand Rapids, MI: Zondervan, 2000), 597.

Epilogue
Good God Is Good!

I had the good fortune of visiting the warm and scenic French Caribbean isle of Guadeloupe on two occasions. Both times, I was there as an invited lecturer on racial justice and reconciliation. I also had the pleasure of preaching on Sundays in local churches. The official language of this Department of France is, of course, French. Most of Guadeloupe's citizens are Black and also speak (and often prefer) Creole. I was the only invited speaker who did not speak French or Creole. I was assigned a team of translators who were English teachers in the island's high schools. They would translate my lectures from English into French. Also, they would sit next to me during the proceedings and softly whisper the English translation of the other speakers' lectures, which were in French. This way I could understand what was presented by my fellow lecturers.

For some of my lectures and all my sermons, Marquise Armand (now Beaupierre) was my translator. She is a teacher of English and a committed woman of the church. This helped us gain a translation rhythm for the preaching that was important for sermon delivery and communication. Marquise also brought a proficiency in Creole. She speaks, studies, and teaches Creole. Her multilingual abilities helped me say a few key words from the local languages in my sermons. The congregations appreciated my attempts to say Jesus as *Jésus* (in French) and *Jezi* (in Creole).

I also asked Marquise to help me say "God" in Creole. What she described, I found fascinating. Let me quote her from an email she sent after I left the island to ensure I remembered her explanation. Marquise wrote, "God in Creole is *Bondyé* [*bon* (like *bonjour*) and *dee'ey* (like when you say 'hey' but don't pronounce the 'h') Bondyé. Bon means good and 'dyé' is God in Creole (in French we say *dieu*). So, God's name in Creole is 'goodgod.' To say God is good, in Creole it goes 'Bondyé bon' = 'Goodgod is good'!! Here you are Mister Preacher!"[1]

I found this so profound. Built into the name of God in Creole is that God is a good God. By definition and name, God is good. Then to say "God is good" in Creole doubles the emphasis on the goodness of God—good God is good. This is an excellent reminder as I close out this book of sermonic reflections for racial justice activists and contemplate the risks of being woke. The deep belief that God is good must be at the core of why we work for racial justice. The world can be harsh and brutal. As I finish writing this book in 2022, I reflect on the killing by police of Amir Locke here in Minneapolis; the killing of Black people in a grocery store in Buffalo; the killing of school children in Uvalde, Texas; and so many more deaths, traumas, and tragedies.

Yet, we must believe that God is good. Our work is motivated by the desire that our world becomes a better reflection of our good God Bondyé. The goodness of God lives in creative tension with a troubled world. Perhaps, we can join poet Mary Oliver each day when we wake up in the midst of troubles and express the gratitude felt in these lines: "Just to be alive, on this fresh morning, in a broken world."[2] The risk of being woke is countered by being awake and aware of the faithfulness and goodness of Bondyé—the core belief in a good God that is eternally good.

Sound the sermonic in a broken world. Work for racial justice in a broken world where the power of the prophet never dies. Build community in a broken world where oppressed lives matter and we are better together. Seek the mystic in a broken world and rest in the womb of God. When the empire strikes back, hear the call

131

out of Egypt and enter God's time zone. Put on the lens of eternity and look past a broken world toward a racially just future yet unseen. Stay woke with the good God who is good! Amen Bondyé!

Notes
1. Email from Marquise Armand, January 31, 2011.
2. Mary Oliver, *Red Bird* (Boston: Beacon Press, 2008), 19.

Appendix

Sermonic Statements for Racial Justice in Minnesota (2020–2022)

Social transformation and movement building has traditionally depended on dynamic orators. The civil rights movement of the 1950s and 1960s in the United States had Martin Luther King, Fannie Lou Hamer, Malcolm X, and many others. In today's racial justice movement, the sermonic can also include spoken word, poetry, song, dance, art, public statements, and the like. What makes it sermonic is its connection to Scripture. To illustrate, below are three sermonic public statements released by the Minnesota Council of Churches after three police killings of Black men. They speak the truth of the prophets, with heartfelt compassion, in the midst of the deaths of George Floyd, Duante Wright, and Amir Locke.

Statement in Response to the Police Killing of George Floyd in Minneapolis

(May 27, 2020) Minneapolis, MN—Rev. Dr. Curtiss Paul DeYoung, CEO of the Minnesota Council of Churches, issued this statement:

The Scriptures often cry out, "How long, O Lord?" This cry is emanating once again from Minneapolis and the rest of the nation with the police killing of George Floyd. Another brutal killing of a Black person by law enforcement. How long, O

God? He was killed while screaming, "Please, I can't breathe."
How long, O God? Three police officers watched, heard the
cry, and did not intervene. How long, O God? How long will
the killing of African Americans by police officers continue?
The brutal attacks on Black bodies is not acceptable. How long,
O God?

In this moment, I ask the faith community for these four responses:

Presence—Find ways to be present where people are feeling
grief and outrage. Many of us were at the protest rally last
night in Minneapolis held at the site of the killing. But this
presence must continue in the days ahead. Reach out to
African American church leaders and members and stand with
them in this moment. Stand with the Minneapolis NAACP,
Urban League, and other Black-led civil rights and community organizations. Stand with the courageous young activists
who have relentlessly pressed the issues through the senseless
police killings of Jamar Clark and Philando Castile and now
George Floyd.

Protest—Presence must turn into protest. Speak truth to power.
Do not allow this great violation to go unchecked. Call for police
accountability. Call for a system-wide transformation of policing in
Minnesota. Call this an act of anti-Black racism even when some
white narratives blame the victim.

Prosecution—Protest is not enough. The four police officers
involved must be charged and prosecuted. Our moral voice must
help ensure this happens.

Prayers—As people of faith we must pray for the family and
friends of George Floyd. We must pray for the neighbors in the
Central Neighborhood of Minneapolis where this great violation
occurred. We must pray for African Americans and People of
Color who are feeling fear, rage, grief, and hopelessness. We must
pray for racial justice and equity in our city and nation.

How long, O God, how long?

Statement in Response to the Police Killing of Daunte Wright in Brooklyn Center

(April 12, 2021) Minneapolis, MN—Presiding Elder Stacey Smith (President), Rev. Dr. Curtiss Paul DeYoung (CEO), and Rev. Jim Bear Jacobs (Director of Racial Justice) of the Minnesota Council of Churches, issued this statement:

The prophet Jeremiah cried out: "A voice is heard in Ramah, mourning and great weeping, Rachel weeping for her children and refusing to be comforted, because her children are no more" (31:15).

Mourning and weeping are heard once again from Minnesota. With the killing of 20-year-old Daunte Wright by a police officer in Brooklyn Center another child is no more. Another baby is destined to grow up without a father. Another mother cannot be comforted. Another Black body unnecessarily killed by a law enforcement officer.

In moments like this our resolve is tested. In our neighborhoods and in our cities, we have not yet processed our grief from last May when George Floyd was killed in the public square, and today the wound in our Black communities is made raw once again.

In this moment, we ask the faith community to respond through:

Prayers—As people of faith we must pray for the family and friends of Daunte Wright who are mourning and weeping. They are mourning for their child Daunte and weeping for his now fatherless child. We must pray for our neighbors in Brooklyn Center where this injustice occurred. We must pray for African Americans and People of Color who are once again feeling fear, rage, grief, and hopelessness. And we must pray for justice in the ongoing trial of former police officer Derek Chauvin who killed George Floyd in Minneapolis. We must pray for racial justice and equity in our city, state, and nation.

Presence—Prayers must become presence. In moments like this, outrage is a natural part of grief, which is best processed in community. We invite you to stand with African American church leaders and members in this moment. Stand with the NAACP, Urban League, and other Black-led civil rights and community organizations. Stand with courageous young activists who have relentlessly pressed the issues through the senseless police killings of Jamar Clark, Philando Castile, George Floyd, and now Daunte Wright.

Prophesy—Presence must turn into prophecy. Refuse to be comforted. Refuse to rationalize this killing. Speak truth to power. Call for police accountability. Call for Minnesota legislators to take action on proposed police reform bills. Call for a system-wide transformation of policing in Minnesota.

Statement in Response to the Police Killing of Amir Locke in Minneapolis

(February 8, 2022) Minneapolis, MN—Presiding Elder Stacey Smith, President; Bishop Richard Howell, Vice President; Rev. Curtiss DeYoung, Chief Executive Officer; Rev. Jim Bear Jacobs, Co-Director of Racial Justice; Rev. Pamela Ngunjiri, Co-Director of Racial Justice of the Minnesota Council of Churches, issued this statement:

No more words . . .

A young Black man, Amir Locke, was killed by Minneapolis police on Wednesday morning, February 2, 2022. Reminiscent of Breonna Taylor, Minneapolis police used a no-knock warrant to silently enter the private residence where he was asleep and they shot and killed Amir. They were looking for someone else.

We have no more words . . . First, we are still numb and in shock. Second, with the police killings of George Floyd and Daunte Wright, we made statements, quoted Scripture, protested, and called for action. Our colleagues around the country who are speaking out about police killings of Black people, Native people, and other People of Color in their communities are also feeling like they have said all that needs to be said already.

We have no more words . . . Yet Amir's family needs our prayers.

We have no more words . . . Yet Black women, many who were mothers, gathered on Monday to cry out for justice, accountability, and the transformation of public safety. So, we must join these courageous Black women and once again find the words, the Scriptures, the protests, and the actions to demand that the City of Minneapolis account for its racism and incompetence in policing. We must demand from the mayor of Minneapolis to use his newly gained powers to transform public safety in Minneapolis. And we use the prophet Isaiah's words to demand, "Learn to do right; seek justice. Defend the oppressed" (1:17).

Bibliography

Akoto, Dorothy Bea (née Abutiate). "Esther." In *The Africana Bible: Reading Israel's Scriptures from Africa and the African Diaspora*, general editor Hugh R. Page Jr., 268–72. Minneapolis: Fortress, 2009.

Anderson, Cheryl B. *Ancient Laws and Contemporary Controversies: The Need for Inclusive Biblical Interpretation.* New York: Oxford University Press, 2009.

Baldwin, Joyce G. *Esther: An Introduction and Commentary.* Downers Grove, IL: InterVarsity Press, 1984.

Beasley-Murray, G. R. *John.* Word Biblical Commentary 36. Waco, TX: Word Books, 1987.

Boesak, Allan Aubrey, and Curtiss Paul DeYoung. *Radical Reconciliation: Beyond Political Pietism and Christian Quietism.* Maryknoll, NY: Orbis Books, 2012.

Borg, Marcus J., and John Dominic Crossan. *The Last Week: A Day-by-Day Account of Jesus's Final Week in Jerusalem.* San Francisco: HarperSanFrancisco, 2006.

Brown, Raymond E. *The Birth of the Messiah: A Commentary on the Infancy Narratives in Matthew and Luke.* Garden City, NY: Image Books, 1979.

———. *The Gospel According to John, I–XII.* Anchor Bible 29. Garden City, NY: Doubleday, 1966.

———. *The Gospel According to John XIII–XXI.* Anchor Yale Bible. New Haven, CT: Yale University Press, 1970.

Brueggemann, Walter. *Genesis.* Interpretation: A Bible Commentary for Teaching and Preaching. Atlanta: John Knox, 1982.

Burrus, Virginia. "The Gospel of Luke and Acts of the Apostles." In *A Postcolonial Commentary on the New Testament Writings*, edited by Fernando F. Segovia and R. S. Sugurtharajah, 133-55. London: T&T Clark, 2009.

Bush, Frederick. *Ruth-Esther*. Word Biblical Commentary 9. Grand Rapids, MI: Zondervan, 1996.

Clarke, Thurston. *The Last Campaign: Robert F. Kennedy and 82 Days that Inspired America*. New York: Henry Holt, 2008.

Copher, Charles B. *Black Biblical Studies: An Anthology of Charles B. Copher*. Chicago: Black Light Fellowship, 1993.

Craddock, Fred B. "The Letter to the Hebrews." In *The New Interpreter's Bible* vol. 12, edited by Leander E. Keck, 1-173. Nashville: Abingdon, 1998.

Crawford, Sidnie White. "The Book of Esther." In *The New Interpreter's Bible* vol. 3, edited by Leander E. Keck, 853-972. Nashville: Abingdon, 1999.

Crossan, John Dominic, and Jonathan L. Reed. *In Search of Paul: How Jesus's Apostle Opposed Rome's Empire with God's Kingdom*. San Francisco: HarperSanFrancisco, 2004.

Culpepper, R. Alan. "The Gospel of Luke." In *The New Interpreter's Bible* vol. 9, edited by Leander E. Keck, 1-490. Nashville: Abingdon, 1995.

Darity, William A., Jr., and A. Kirsten Mullen. *From Here to Equality: Reparations for Black Americans in the Twenty-First Century*. Chapel Hill: University of North Carolina Press, 2020.

De La Torre, Miguel A. *Genesis*. Belief: A Theological Commentary on the Bible. Louisville, KY: Westminster John Knox, 2011.

————. *The Politics of Jesús: A Hispanic Political Theology*. Lanham, MD: Rowman & Littlefield, 2015.

Dennis, Marie, Renny Golden, and Scott Wright. *Oscar Romero: Reflections on His Life and Writings*. Maryknoll, NY: Orbis Books, 2000.

DeYoung, Curtiss Paul. *Coming Together in the Twenty-First Century: The Bible's Message in an Age of Diversity.* Valley Forge, PA: Judson Press, 2009.

———. *Homecoming: A "White" Man's Journey through Harlem to Jerusalem.* Eugene, OR: Wipf & Stock, 2009, 2015.

———. *Living Faith: How Faith Inspires Social Justice.* Minneapolis: Fortress, 2007.

———. "Race and Policing in America." *Chicago Tribune,* November 24, 2014. www.chicagotribune.com/opinion/commentary/ct-ferguson-police-michael-brown-darren-wilson-black-men-whites-perspec-1125-20141125-story.html.

DeYoung, Curtiss Paul, Wilda C. Gafney, Leticia A. Guardiola-Sáenz, George ("Tink") Tinker, and Frank M. Yamada, eds. *The Peoples' Bible: New Revised Standard Version with Apocrypha.* Minneapolis: Fortress, 2008.

DeYoung, Curtiss Paul, Jacqueline J. Lewis, Micky ScottBey Jones, Robyn Afrik, Sarah Thompson Nahar, Sindy Morales Garcia, and 'Iwalani Ka'ai. *Becoming Like Creoles: Living and Leading at the Intersections of Injustice, Culture, and Religion.* Minneapolis: Fortress, 2019.

Dunn, James D. G. *Romans 9–16.* Word Biblical Commentary 38B. Grand Rapids, MI: Zondervan, 1988.

Elliot, Neil. "The Apostle Paul and Empire." In *In the Shadow of Empire: Reclaiming the Bible as a History of Faithful Resistance,* edited by Richard A. Horsley, 97–116. Louisville, KY: Westminster John Knox, 2008.

———. *Liberating Paul: The Justice of God and the Politics of the Apostle.* Minneapolis: Fortress, 2006.

Equal Justice Initiative. *Lynching in America: Confronting the Legacy of Racial Terror.* Montgomery, AL: Equal Justice Initiative, 2017.

Fallon, Ivan. "CIA Admits: We Sent Mandela to Jail." *The Sunday Times* (UK), May 15, 2016. www.thetimes.co.uk/

article/cia-tip-off-led-to-jailing-of-mandela-9mwcsdq9c.

Felder, Cain Hope, ed. *The Original African Heritage Study Bible—King James Version*. Nashville: James C. Winston, 1993.

———, ed. *Stony the Road We Trod: African American Biblical Interpretation—Thirtieth Anniversary Expanded Edition*. Minneapolis: Fortress, 2021.

———. *Troubling Biblical Waters: Race, Class, and Family*. Maryknoll, NY: Orbis Books, 1989.

France, R. T. *The Gospel of Matthew*. New International Commentary on the New Testament. Grand Rapids, MI: Eerdmans, 2007.

Gafney, Wilda C. *A Woman's Lectionary for the Whole Church: A Multi-Gospel Single-Year Lectionary*. New York: Church Publishing, 2021.

González, Justo L. *For the Healing of the Nations: The Book of Revelation in an Age of Cultural Conflict*. Maryknoll, NY: Orbis Books, 1999.

Guelich, Robert A. *Mark 1–8:26*. Word Biblical Commentary 34A. Dallas: Word Books, 1989.

Gundry, R. H. *Mark: A Commentary on His Apology for the Cross*. Grand Rapids, MI: Eerdmans, 1993.

Hall, Stuart. "Créolité and the Process of Creolization." In *The Creolization Reader: Studies in Mixed Identities and Cultures*, edited by Robin Cohen and Paola Toninto, 26–38. London: Routledge, 2010.

Hall, Tony. "Tony Hall's Interview with Nelson Mandela in Hiding." *Ars Notoria*, September 10, 2020. www.arsnotoria.com/2020/09/10/tony-halls-interview-with-nelson-mandela-in-hiding.

Hiebert, Theodore. *The Beginning of Difference: Discovering Identity in God's Diverse World*. Nashville: Abingdon, 2019.

Horsley, Richard A., ed. *In the Shadow of Empire: Reclaiming the Bible as a History of Faithful Resistance*. Louisville, KY: Westminster John Knox, 2008.

————. *Jesus and Empire: The Kingdom of God and the New World Disorder*. Minneapolis: Fortress, 2003.

Ingraham, Christopher. "Racial Inequality in Minneapolis among the Worst in the Nation." *Washington Post*, May 30, 2020. https://www.washingtonpost.com/business/2020/05/30/minneapolis-racial-inequality/.

Ingram, Jessica Kendall. "How to Handle the Silence of God." *The African American Pulpit* 6, no. 2 (Spring 2003): 47–50.

Jennings, Willie James. *Acts*. Belief: A Theological Commentary on the Bible. Louisville, KY: Westminster John Knox, 2017.

————. *The Christian Imagination: Theology and the Origins of Race*. New Haven, CT: Yale University Press, 2010.

Johnson, Kimberly P. *The Womanist Preacher: Proclaiming Womanist Rhetoric from the Pulpit*. London: Lexington Books, 2017.

Johnson, Luke Timothy. *The First and Second Letter to Timothy*. Anchor Yale Bible 35A. New Haven, CT: Yale University Press, 2001, 2008.

Jones, Robert P. *White Too Long: The Legacy of White Supremacy in American Christianity*. New York: Simon & Schuster, 2020.

Lane, William L. *Hebrews 9–13*. Word Biblical Commentary 47B. Nashville: Thomas Nelson, 1991.

Lewis, Jacqueline J. *The Power of Stories: A Guide for Leading Multi-Racial and Multi-Cultural Congregations*. Nashville: Abingdon, 2008.

Linn, Otto F. *The Gospel of John*. Anderson, IN: Gospel Trumpet Company, 1942.

Malina, Bruce J., and Richard L. Rohrbaugh. *Social Science Commentary on the Gospel of John*. Minneapolis: Fortress, 1998.

————. *Social Science Commentary on the Synoptic Gospels*. Minneapolis: Fortress, 1992.

Massey, James Earl. *Preaching from Hebrews: Hermeneutical*

Insights and Homiletical Helps. Anderson, IN: Warner Press, 2014.

———. *Views from the Mountain: Select Writings of James Earl Massey*. Edited by Barry L. Callen and Curtiss Paul DeYoung. Glendora, CA: Aldersgate Press, 2018.

Michaels, J. Ramsey. *The Gospel of John*. New International Commentary on the New Testament. Grand Rapids, MI: Eerdmans, 2010.

Morris, Leon L. *The Gospel According to John*. New International Commentary on the New Testament. Grand Rapids, MI: Eerdmans, 1971.

———. *The Gospel According to Matthew*. Pillar New Testament Commentary. Grand Rapids, MI: Eerdmans, 1992.

Mounce, William D. *Pastoral Epistles*. Word Biblical Commentary 46. Grand Rapids, MI: Zondervan, 2000.

Nandos, Mark D. *The Irony of Galatians: Paul's Letter in First-Century Context*. Minneapolis: Fortress, 2002.

O'Day, Gail R. "The Gospel of John." In *The New Interpreter's Bible* vol. 9, edited by Leander E. Keck, 491-865. Nashville: Abingdon, 1995.

Oliver, Mary. *Red Bird*. Boston: Beacon Press, 2008.

Page, Hugh R., Jr., general editor. *The Africana Bible: Reading Israel's Scriptures from Africa and the African Diaspora*. Minneapolis: Fortress, 2009.

Pollard, Alton B., III. *Mysticism and Social Change: The Social Witness of Howard Thurman*. New York: Peter Lang, 1992.

Rice, Gene. *Africa and the Bible: Corrective Lenses*. Eugene, OR: Cascade Books, 2019.

Sadler, Rodney S., Jr. "Genesis." In *The Africana Bible: Reading Israel's Scriptures from Africa and the African Diaspora*, general editor Hugh R. Page Jr., 70–79. Minneapolis: Fortress, 2010.

Sarna, Nahum M. *Genesis*. The JPS Torah Commentary. Philadelphia: The Jewish Publication Society, 1989.

Sechrest, Love L. "'Humbled Among the Nations': Matthew 15:21-28 in Anti-Racist Womanist Missiological Engagement." In *Can "White" People Be Saved? Triangulating Race, Theology, and Mission*, edited by Love L. Sechrest, Johnny Ramírez-Johnson, and Amos Young, 276-99. Downers Grove, IL: IVP Academic, 2018.

Sechrest, Love L., Johnny Ramírez-Johnson, and Amos Young, eds. *Can "White" People Be Saved? Triangulating Race, Theology, and Mission*. Downers Grove, IL: IVP Academic, 2018.

Sidorenko, Konstantin. *Robert F. Kennedy: A Spiritual Biography*. New York: Crossroad, 2000.

Smith, Mitzi J., Angela N. Parker, and Ericka S. Dunbar Hill, eds. *Bitter the Chastening Rod: Africana Biblical Interpretation after Stony the Road We Trod in the Age of BLM, SayHerName, and MeToo*. Lanham, MD: Lexington Books/Fortress Academic, 2022.

Sone, Isaiah. "Synagogue." In *The Interpreter's Dictionary of the Bible: An Illustrated Encyclopedia, R–Z*, ed. George Arthur Buttrick, 479–91. Nashville: Abingdon, 1962.

Stengel, Richard. *Mandela's Way: Fifteen Lessons on Life, Love, and Courage*. New York: Crown, 2009.

Thompson, Marianne Meye. *John: A Commentary*. New Testament Library. Louisville, KY: Westminster John Knox, 2015.

Thurman, Howard. *The Inward Journey: Meditations on the Spiritual Quest*. New York: Harper & Brothers, 1961.

———. *Meditations for Apostles of Sensitiveness*. Mills College, CA: Eucalyptus Press, 1948.

———. *Mysticism and the Experience of Love*. Wallingford, PA: Pendle Hill Pamphlet 115, 1961.

Wall, Robert W. "The Acts of the Apostles." In *The New Interpreter's Bible* vol. 10, edited by Leander E. Keck, 1–368. Nashville: Abingdon, 2002.

Washington, James M., ed. *A Testament of Hope: The Essential Writings and Speeches of Martin Luther King Jr.* San Francisco: HarperSanFrancisco, 1986.

Wenham, Gordan J. *Genesis 1–15.* Word Biblical Commentary 1. Grand Rapids, MI: Zondervan, 1987.

Woodley, Randy S. *Shalom and the Community of Creation: An Indigenous Vision.* Grand Rapids, MI: Eerdmans, 2012.

Wildman, Terry *First Nations Version: An Indigenous Translation of the New Testament.* Downers Grove, IL: InterVarsity Press, 2021.

Wright, Jeremiah A., Jr. *What Makes You So Strong?: Sermons of Joy and Strength.* Edited by Jini Kilgore Ross. Valley Forge, PA: Judson Press, 1993.

Wright, N. T. "The Letter to the Romans." In *The New Interpreter's Bible* vol. 10, edited by Leander E. Keck, 393–770. Nashville: Abingdon, 2002.